Anonymous

Worcester Family Cook Book

Anonymous
Worcester Family Cook Book
ISBN/EAN: 9783744792080
Printed in Europe, USA, Canada, Australia, Japan
Cover: Foto ©Andreas Hilbeck / pixelio.de

More available books at **www.hansebooks.com**

Cheapest place in Worcester to buy your CLOAKS AND FURS is the
PARIS CLOAK AND SUIT STORE, 496 Main Street.

WORCESTER

FAMILY

COOK BOOK

"THE HOUSEWIFE'S AID."

RECIPES
...OF THE
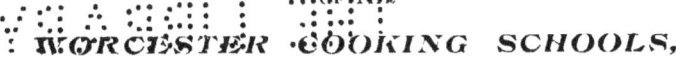
WORCESTER COOKING SCHOOLS,

To which are appended other Choice Recipes.

THE MAGEE GRAND.

Was awarded the GOLD MEDAL at the WORLD'S FAIR.

The OVEN is thoroughly and scientifically ventilated.

It has an OVEN THERMOMETER which has been pronounced by professionals the greatest aid to good cooking of any invention of recent years.

MISS PARLOA uses and recommends Magee Ranges as the best.

J. W. JORDAN, 609 & 611 Main St., WORCESTER.

HAS SOLD MAGEE GOODS FORTY-THREE YEARS.

LE JOLLY DYE HOUSE, 326 Main St. and 89 Exchange St.
Dyes and Cleanses in the best manner.
C. T MELVIN, Proprietor

SOUP A l'ITALIENNE.

1-2 onion.
1 tablespoonful butter.
1 tablespoonful butter.
1 1-2 pints hot stock
3 yolks of eggs.
Salt and pepper to taste.

Bring the stock to a boil. Heat the cream in a double boiler. Melt the butter, add the flour, salt, pepper and onion juice and stir into the hot stock. Strain on the cream stirring constantly. Beat the eggs and put them into the tureen. Pour hot soup over the egg, stirring. Serve at once with grated cheese.

CRECY SOUP.

1 pt. raw carrots.
Two tablespoonfuls butter.
1 qt. white stock.
1 blade mace.
1 teaspoonful salt.
1 spoonful white pepper.
1 tablespoonful butter.
1 tablespoonful corn starch.
1 cup hot cream.

Cook the carrots, cut fine, in butter, twenty minutes, somewhat soft, add to 1-4 soup stock, mace, pepper and salt. Simmer thirty minutes, strain. Melt butter, add corn starch. blend, pour on the hot stock slowly, stirring. Add the hot cream, strain again. Serve with croutons.

BAKED BEAN SOUP.

1 pint cold baked beans.
1 pint cold water.
1-2 as much tomato.
Water, salt, pepper, Mustard, thickening.

Add the cold water to the beans and simmer until soft, strain, add half as much strained tomato as you have liquid. Melt butter, add flour, salt and pepper. Blend thoroughly, add mustard and hot liquid slowly, stirring. Serve with fried croutons.

RICHARD HEALY. - 512 Main Street.
Furs, Cloaks, Suits, Mackintoshes and Silk Waists.

THE WORCESTER
Mechanics Savings Bank.

311 MAIN STREET.

Deposits commence interest on the 15th day of January, April, July and October.

BANK HOURS.
9 A. M. to 4 P. M.   Saturdays, 9 A. M. to 1 P. M.

J. EDWIN SMITH, President.
HENRY WOODWARD, Treasurer.

Worcester, April 6, 1892.

C. L. BLAIR, Photographer,
Studio, Chase Building.
Use Elevator
44 FRONT STREET, WORCESTER, MASS.

SALMON SOUP.

1-2 can salmon.
1 quart milk.
1 slice onion.
1 tablespoonful butter.
2 teaspoonfuls salt.
1 teaspoonful pepper.

Pu the milk in a double boiler to heat with the slice of onion. Melt the butter and stir in flour, pepper and salt and add to the hot milk. Drain the salmon thoroughly in a colander, picking out the skin and bones. Put the fish through a vegetable strainer. Put the salmon into the milk and stand on the back of the stove half an hour, to draw out the salmon flavor.

POULETTE SOUP.

3 pints milk.
3 tablespoonfuls butter.
3 tablespoonfuls flour.
3 tablespoonfuls onion.
3 tablespoonfuls carrot.
3 tablespoonfuls turnip.
Sprig of parsley.
Bay leaf.
1-2 blade mace.
1 cup cream.
Yolks four eggs.
1 teaspoonful salt.

Heat the mace, parsley and bay leaf in the milk. Cook the chopped vegetables in the butter twenty minutes, stirring so as not to burn them. Add the flour and the hot milk slowly. Cook in a double boiler thirty minutes. Beat the eggs thoroughly, add cold cream and add to the soup, cook one minute, serve hot,

POTATO SOUP.

3 large potatoes.
1 pint milk.
1 tablespoonful chopped onion.
1 teaspoonful salt.
1-2 tablespoonful butter.
A little celery salt.

Cook the flour in the butter, add seasoning to mashed potato. Heat the milk with the onion in it, pour into flour and butter and gradually add to the potato, beating very thoroughly. Strain through a colander, cook a few minutes, serve hot. Hot cream may be added the last thing

Mrs. Bowen's School of Elocution and Delsarte,
34 FRONT ST., WORCESTER, MASS.

E. T. SMITH & CO.'S SPICES, in Tin Boxes

are used and recommended by Mrs. C. E. Humphrey, Teacher of Cooking School.

ONION SOUP.

1 tablespoonful butter.
2 or 3 onions.
1-4 cup flour.
1 pint boiling water.
Salt and pepper.
A quart or less of milk.
2 or 3 mashed potatoes.

Melt the butter, add 2 or 3 large onions, chopped fine, cook until browned. Brown in a hot pan 1-4 cup of flour, add to butter, with salt and pepper. Stir in one pint boiling water, add the potato and one quart hot milk. Serve with browned crackers.

BAKING POWDER ROLLS.

1 quart pastry flour.
1 teaspoonful shortening.
1 scant teaspoonful salt.
3 teaspoonfuls baking powder.
Milk to moisten.

Mix the dry ingredients and sift them thoroughly, add milk gradually, working up with a knife, until stiff to handle. Roll out and cut in rounds. Spread with melted butter and fold together, rise fifteen minutes, bake on tin sheets.

PARKER HOUSE ROLLS.

White of one egg.
1 pint sweet milk.
1 tablespoonful butter, melted.
1 teaspoonful salt.
1 tablespoonful sugar.
1-2 yeast cake, dissolved in a little water.
Flour to make a stiff dough.

Beat the white of one egg stiff. Heat the milk lukewarm in a double boiler, add melted butter, salt and sugar, and yeast. Pour in the egg and flour, until ready to knead. Knead carefully until the dough feels springy. Set to rise ten or twelve hours.

One trial of **Baker's Pure Extract of Vanilla** will convince you that it is absolutely pure and of the greatest strength attainable without the use of poisonous chemicals

Peoples Savings Bank,

452 MAIN ST., WORCESTER, MASS.

Incorporated May 13, 1864.

DEPOSITS, JANUARY, 1895, . $6,685,320.52.
GUARANTY FUND, . . . 230,000.00.

Deposits put upon interest on the first day of February, May, August and November.

Semi-annual dividends are payable February and August 15th, and added to the principal, if not withdrawn.

All Taxes paid by the bank.

Bank hours from 9 to 4. Saturday, 9 to and 6 to 8.

SAM'L R. HEYWOOD, Pres.   CHARLES M. BENT, Treas.

WORCESTER
Five Cents Savings Bank,

No. 314 MAIN STREET.

Incorporated, April 1, 1854.

Deposits put on interest on the first day of January, April, July and October.

All taxes on deposits paid by the bank.

BANK HOURS—9 a. m. to 4 p. m. Saturdays, 9 a. m. to 1 p. m.

F. B. STODDARD, Pres.   J. STEWART BROWN, Treas.

E. T. SMITH & CO.'S SPICES in Tin Boxes

are used and recommended by Mrs. C. E. Humphrey, Teacher of Cooking School.

OMELETTE.

3 eggs.
3 tablespoonfuls milk.
1 teaspoonful salt.
Speck of pepper.

Separate the eggs, beat the yolks thick and creamy, add milk, salt and pepper. Beat the whites perfectly dry and stiff; cut them into the yolks. Put a tablespoonful of butter into a frying pan; when bubbling, pour in the mixture, let stand until it sets, on top of stove, then place in the oven on the grate until done, in a moderate oven. Fold over, serve at once.

A tablespoonful of the white of an egg beaten out on the last thing, makes snow omelette.

SCOTCH EGGS.

1 cup ham.
7 eggs.
1-3 cup milk.
1-3 cup bread crumbs.
Speck cayenne.

Boil six eggs hard, make bread crumbs to a smooth paste in hot milk, mix this with a cup of chopped ham and one raw egg, slightly beaten, cayenne, and half teaspoonful mustard, if there is none in the ham. Take off shells and cover with the paste and roll in dry crumbs. Place in a wire basket and fry in hot fat, cut in two and lay on a bed of parsley, on a platter.

Take canned deviled ham.

WELSH RAREBIT.

2 cups grated cheese.
2-3 cup milk.
1 teaspoonful mustard.
1 teaspoonful salt.
2 teaspoonfuls butter.
2 eggs.

Cheese, milk, mustard and cayenne in a double boiler, add butter and beaten eggs; cook two minutes. Serve hot on moistened toast in triangles.

L. CURRIER, Real Estate & Mortgage Loans
405 MAIN ST., WORCESTER, MASS.

C. L. Gorham & Co.

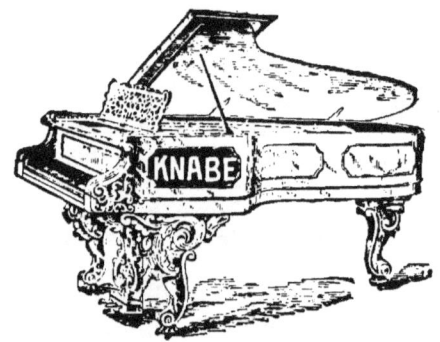

DEALERS IN
FINE PIANOS,

Among which prominently appears the

Which has for over fifty years maintained its unpurchased pre-eminence, as well as an unsolicited endorsement from the greatest artists of both worlds.

We have furnished Pianos for seven successive Music Festivals, and at all Symphony and other high class Concerts given here. Pianos moved, tuned and repaired in city or county. Sheet Music and Musical Merchandise in great variety.

C. L. GORHAM & CO., 454 MAIN STREET.

E. T. SMITH & CO.'S SPICES, in Tin Boxes

are used and recommended by Mrs. C. E. Humphrey, Teacher of Cooking School.

CHEESE SOUFFLE.

2 tablespoonfuls butter.
1 tablespoonful flour,
1-2 cup milk.
1 cup grated cheese.

3 eggs beaten separately.
1-2 teaspoonful salt.
Speck of cayenne.

Heat butter, add flour and seasoning, stir until thick, add milk, cook two minutes, add well beaten yolks of eggs and cheese, then carefully cut in stiff whites. Bake in a quick oven twenty minutes.

May be made with potato instead of cheese.

HALIBUT AU GRATIN.

2 lbs. halibut.
2 teaspoonfuls butter.
2 teaspoonfuls flour.
Juice half lemon.

1 pint brown stock
canned consomme.
1 teaspoonful pepper.
1 teaspoonful salt.

Remove skin and bone. Cut the fish in small squares, make a brown sauce of butter, flour and soup stock, with salt and pepper and lemon juice. Butter an earthen dish, put in a layer of fish, half the sauce. Repeat and cover with prepared bread crumbs. Bake in a moderate oven forty minutes.

BROILED OYSTERS.

Use one pint large oysters. Dry in a cloth. Melt a piece of butter in a stew pan and place the oysters in it for a little while. Roll in sifted bread crumbs, season with salt and pepper and broil from two to five minutes in a broiler with wire close together.

Baker's Extract of Vanilla is made by a new and original process, being free from the alcoholic odors and taste found in all other brands.

THE "GLENWOOD"

should be critically examined, to fully comprehend its many points of excellence.

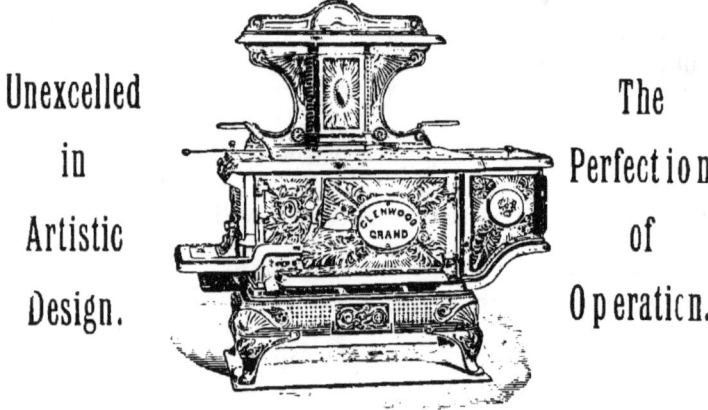

Unexcelled in Artistic Design.

The Perfection of Operation.

GLENWOOD GRAND.

Indorsed by a host of Worcester ladies, and the strongest guarantee ever given, by

O. S. KENDALL & CO.

E. T. SMITH & CO.'S SPICES, in Tin Boxes,

are used and recommended by Mrs. C. E. Humphrey, Teacher of Cooking School.

FRENCH CHOPS.

Butter common letter paper, and fold over a chop. Broil about six minutes over a clear fire, carefully turning so as not to set fire to the paper. Salt and serve at once on a hot platter.

CHICKEN SOUFFLE.

1 cup white sauce.
1 teaspoonful chopped parsley.
A few drops onion juice.
1 cup chopped meat.
2 eggs.

Open a can of chicken, measure one cup of meat after it is chopped. add beaten yolks of eggs, parsley, white sauce, and last of all fold in the stiffly beaten whites of eggs. Bake in an earthen dish and serve hot in the same dish.

WHITE SAUCE.—1 cup milk, 1 tablespoonful butter, 1 tablespoonful flour, salt and pepper.

Melt the butter, add flour and seasoning, slowly add the milk, stir all the time.

SCALLOPED ONIONS.

6 onions.
1 tablespoonful butter.
1 1-2 cups hot milk.
Salt and pepper.
1 cup bread crumbs.
1-3 cup butter melted for the bread crumbs.

Boil onions ten minutes, change the water, ten minutes more, change again, cook about thirty minutes in salted water.

Quarter the onions, pour over them a thin, white sauce (plus one tablespoonful cheese). Cover with buttered crumbs. brown in a quick oven.

Baker's Non-Alcoholic G nger, An unfailing remedy for Colds, Cramps, Colic, Chills, Diarrhœa, and all forms of Summer Complaint.

The Right Thing on the Wall

are our new designs, brilliant and pleasing as the fascinations of the magic lantern to happy school children.

Our victorious display of new designs in Wall Paper presents a three-fold surprise of variety, elegance and cheapness. Wall Paper designing is now a fine art, and artists of the highest ability are engaged in producing the masterpieces of beauty and taste seen in our collection. We know what has been produced, and from what has been produced we select the cream to make up our stock. This fact accounts for our success in treating our patrons to a chain of unexpected first choices. Come and choose.

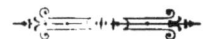

E. G. HIGGINS CO.,

284 MAIN STREET,   Opp. Bay State House.

E. T. SMITH & CO.'S SPICES, in Tin Boxes, are used and recommended by Mrs. C. E. Humphrey, Teacher of Cooking School.

HOLLANDAISE SAUCE.
(For the baked fish).

1 tablespoonful vinegar.	Yolks of four eggs.
6 peppercorns.	4 oz. butter.
1-4 teaspoonful salt.	3 oz butter.

Four tablespoonfuls vinegar in a small sauce pan with the six pepper corns, boil down one-half, cool and add to well beaten yolks of four eggs and four ounces of butter, stir over a very slow fire until creamy. Set in a pan of hot water and stir until light, adding slowly little bits of the three ounces of butter. Pour around fish.

BAKED FISH.

Take any white fish weighing about three pounds. Remove head, skin and bones, halve. Drain and wipe the oysters and dip each in prepared bread crumbs. Lay one-half of fish on a buttered cloth in baking tin, lay on the oysters as dipped, cover with the other half of fish and smother in about one cup of bread crumbs. Bake about forty minutes.

Take one-third cup butter to one cup bread crumbs for the prepared crumbs.

FISH SOUFFLE.

1 cup thick white sauce.	2 eggs.
Onion juice.	1-2 cup flaked fish.
1 teaspoonful chopped parsley.	

Separate the eggs and add the beaten yolks to the fish, then the parsley in the white sauce, and lastly the stiff whites are cut in, bake twenty minutes. Serve in the same dish.

Baker's Vegetable Colors, Red, Green and Yellow are made by our own process, and are perfectly harmless for coloring frostings, confections, etc.

Baker, Witherell & Co.,

SUCCESSORS TO ZEBINA SMALL,

Wholesale and Retail Dealers in all kinds of

Fresh Fish, Oysters and Lobsters.

Also, Planters, Wholesalers and Retailers of

CHOICE BRANDS OF OYSTERS.

NO. 201-2 PLEASANT ST.,

WORCESTER, MASS.

Orders called for. Also by Telephone, No. 440

WHOLESALE FISH DEPARTMENT, 10 T WHARF, BOSTON.

E. T. SMITH & CO.'S SPICES, in Tin Boxes,

are used and recommended by Mrs. C. E. Humphrey, Teacher of Cooking School.

POTATO CROQUETTES.

2 cups cold potato.
1 tablespoonful melted butter.
2 eggs.

Salt and pepper.
1 egg to roll them in.
Sifted bread crumbs.

Mash potato with salt and pepper, add well beaten eggs, (more salt and pepper if needed), form in cylinders. Roll in egg beaten with one tablespoonful of water. Roll in bread crumbs, fry in hot cottolene in a wire basket.

TOMATO FRITTERS.

1 quart can tomatoes.
1 tablespoonful butter.
1 tablespoonful flour.
1 teaspoonful salt.

1 teaspoonful sugar.
1 teaspoonful pepper.
2 eggs.
1 pint sifted crumbs.

Cook the tomatoes ten minutes, add the sugar, make a sauce of butter and flour, salt and pepper. Beat the eggs and stir in but do not cook. Strain into a nappie. Cut eight slices of bread one-half inch thick and lay on a platter with half the sauce in it first, and pour the other half on. Soak one-half hour, cover the slices with crumbs, and fry in a wire basket.

SAVORY RICE.

1 cup rice.
1 1-2 cup stock.
1 cup tomato.
1 teaspoonful salt.

Speck pepper.
1 tablespoonful chopped onion.
2 tablespoonful butter.

Wash rice and put into stock, water or tomato liquor, cook three-quarters of an hour in a double boiler, season with salt and pepper; just before serving a tablespoonful of chopped parsley may be added and the melted butter. If you want onion, cook it with the rice.

WILLIAM GARBUTT & CO. We can Sell or Exchange your REAL ESTATE, Right away
115 WALKER BUILDING. Open Evenings.

C. V. PUTNAM, President. A. B. R. SPRAGUE, Treasurer.

PUTNAM & SPRAGUE CO.,
Furniture and Carpets,
DRAPERIES AND UPHOLSTERY GOODS,
Baby Carriages and Refrigerators.

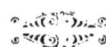

    Our warerooms have more than an acre of floor space.
    Our stock of Furniture is the largest in the city of Worcester.
    Our Carpet Hall is on the street floor.
    We have a good line of Draperies and Upholstery Goods.
    We make our Hair Mattresses and do Fine Upholstery Work.
    We carry a select line of Baby Carriages.
    We have the exclusive sale of the best Refrigerator made.
    We buy for cash, save all discounts, and share them with our customers.
    Please inspect our goods and compare prices. We know that we cannot be undersold.

E. T. SMITH & CO.'S SPICES, in Tin Boxes

are used and recommended by Mrs. C. E. Humphrey, Teacher of Cooking School.

PLAIN PASTRY.

1 heaping cup pastry flour.
1 teaspoonful baking powder.
1 teaspoonful salt.
2 tablespoonfuls shortening.
Cold water.

Sift baking powder and salt into the flour, rub in one tablespoonful butter, cut in water, turn out on a well floured board, roll lightly from you, dot with half the remaining butter, roll, repeat. Put in a cool place.

SHORTCAKE.

2 cups flour.
1-2 cup butter.
1 cup sweet milk.
1 teaspoonful salt.
2 tablespoons baking powder.

Rub butter into flour, into which is sifted the baking powder and salt, add the milk slowly. Roll out to fit jelly cake tins. Mash berries and sugar to put between, and sift powdered sugar on top.

LEMON PIE.

1 cup sugar.
2 eggs.
3 tablespoonfuls flour.
Juice and rind of one lemon.
1 cup boiling water.

Mix sugar, flour, yolks of eggs, lemon juice, add boiling water slowly, stirring, in a double boiler, until like a thin custard, pour into a pastry shell and bake. Make a meringue of whites and two tablespoonfuls of powdered sugar, and brown in open oven.

For Purity, Strength and Delicious Flavor,
BAKER'S EXTRACTS cannot be equaled.

Barnard, Sumner & Putnam Co.
FAMOUS TABLE LINEN SPECIALTIES.

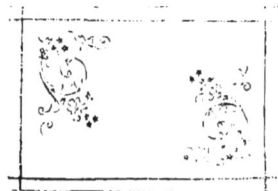

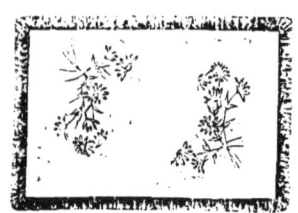

25 CENTS EACH.
Our 25 cent Tray Cloths, universally worth 37½ cents, for 'tis pure linen, hemstitched (size 18 x 27 inches), and stamped in twelve artistic designs, to be worked similar to above. Mailed, postage paid, to any address upon receipt of 27 cents. At 50 cents, 62½ cents and 75 cents, we have Tray Cloths of the very finest linen. Square or oblong shapes.

12½ CENTS EACH.
Our famous 12½ cent Damask Linen Tray Cloths, stamped in twelve designs. The beautiful Damask ground effect does not show in this cut. This is a cloth of the size (18 x 27 inches) and quality that is generally sold at from 17 cents to 25 cents each. We hold the exclusive right for the sale of this Tray Cloth in our territory, and we will send them to any address in the United States, upon the receipt of price, 12½ cents and 2 cents for postage.

Fine Overgaiters and Leggins.

Special attention given to Custom Work. Handsome line of colors for Spring and Summer wear. Call and see them.

Contractor for Making Button Holes in Shoes and Clothing and General Shoe Stitching.

GAITER SUPPLIES FOR SALE.

187 FRONT ST.

E. T. SMITH & CO.'S SPICES in Tin Boxes,
are used and recommended by Mrs. C. E. Humphrey, Teacher of Cooking School.

LEMON SAUCE.

2 cups hot water.   Juice and rind of one lemon.
1 cup sugar.   1 tablespoonful or more butter
2 tablespoonfuls corn starch.

Mix corn starch and sugar thoroughly together, add water, boil five minutes, stirring constantly, add rind and juice of lemon and butter, may stand in a dish of hot water.

PRUNE PUDDING.

1-4 pound prunes.   1-2 tablespoon cream tartar.
5 tablespoons powdered sugar.   5 eggs.

Prunes stewed, stoned and quartered. Separate eggs, beat the whites stiff, sift in sugar and cream tartar, spread 1-2 mixture in a buttered tin dish and put in half the prunes, half the remaining mixture, the rest of the prunes, and cover with the egg left. Bake in a very moderate oven 22 minutes.

CUSTARD.
(For Prune Pudding.)

Beat the yolks of eggs with a pinch of salt, and slowly add a pint of scalded milk, four or five tablespoonfuls sifted sugar, (and vanilla to taste when it has cooled a little). Place the pudding on a platter and pour the custard around it.

ARROWROOT PUDDING.

2 teaspoonfuls arrowroot.   1 teaspoonful powdered sugar.
1 cup cold milk.   Yolks 2 eggs.

Mix arrowroot smooth, add well beaten eggs and sugar. Bake in an earthen pudding bowl, set in a dish of hot water fifteen or twenty minutes.

Tenement Property, COTTAGES AND FARMS, Bought, Sold and Exchanged promptly
WILLIAM GARBUTT & CO, 115 Walker Building,

HORACE KENDALL & SONS,

RETAIL DEALERS IN

Furniture, Carpets, Ranges,

AND ALL KINDS OF

HOUSE FURNISHING GOODS.

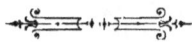

STORES, 319 and rear part of store, with basements, 323 MAIN STREET,
MECHANIC'S HALL BUILDING.

Giving us about 10,000 square feet of flooring.

We keep a large stock of New Furniture of excellent quality constantly on hand, and will sell at as low a price as any house in New England. Our desire is to please all who will favor us with their patronage.

Give us a trial, when in want of anything in the Furniture line.

I. L. CURRIER, REAL ESTATE AND MORTGAGE LOANS,
405 MAIN ST., WORCESTER, MASS.

PLUM PORRIDGE.

(Sometimes called gruel.)

2 dozen raisins.
2 cups milk.

1 tablespoonful flour.
Salt.

Wash, quarter and stew the water out of large raisins, add to cold milk in double boiler. Rub the flour smooth in a little cold milk, add gradually, cook ten minutes, salt, strain, serve hot.

CABINET PUDDING.

1 cup raisins.
1 1-2 cup hot milk.
Yolks 2 eggs.

3 tablespoonfuls sugar.
1-2 teaspoonful salt.
1 quart grated bread.

Grate fresh bread (1 day old) without the crust, butter a pudding mold, decorate with the raisins (boiled five minutes and stoned) then put in a layer of crumbs, alternate until the mo'd is full, beat the yolks, add salt, sugar and hot milk, gradually stirring. Pour this over bread and raisins, cover tightly, cook one hour in a kettle of boiling water, serve hot with Foamy Egg Sauce.

FOAMY EGG SAUCE.

2 eggs.
2 cups powdered sugar.

1 tablespoonful hot milk.
2 tablespoonfuls vanilla.

Beat the eggs thoroughly, add powdered sugar, gradually stirring, add hot milk as you need it. The last thing add vanilla and serve immediately.

Baker's Extracts were awarded First Prize, over eight competitors at the Pure Food Exposition.

LESSONS IN DRESS CUTTING

AT THE

WORCESTER

Dress Cutting School.

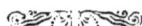

For a thorough course in Dress Cutting and making, $15.00.

Lessons are given every day.

Pupils are instructed separately and not in classes.

The number of lessons is not limited.

Pupils learn on their own work.

Competent help employed in the dress making department.

Cutting and Basting a specialty.

Patterns exhibited and cut to order.

For further particulars, apply to

MRS. L. F. WALCH,

45 PLEASANT STREET.

E. T. SMITH & CO.'S SPICES in Tin Boxes,

are used and recommended by Mrs. C. E. Humphrey, Teacher of Cooking School.

CREAM ALMOND CAKE.

1-2 cup butter.
1 cup powdered sugar.
Whites of four eggs.
2 cups flour.
1 teaspoonful baking powder.
1-2 cup milk.
1-2 teaspoonful almond flavor.

Cream the butter, add sugar gradually, cream thoroughly, sift flour and baking powder together, add milk and flour alternately, add flavor, cut in stiff whites. Bake in two layers.

ORANGE SHERBET.

1 tablespoonful gelatine.
1-2 cup cold water.
1 cup sugar.
1-2 cup boiling water.
1 cup cold water.
6 oranges.
2 lemons.

Put the gelatine into the cold water, ten minutes, dissolve in boiling water, add the sugar to the juice (a scant pint) and one cup cold water, stir in the gelatine, strain into the freezer. Pack in salt and ice, three-quarters ice and one quarter salt.

ALMOND CREAM.

1 cup sugar.
1-2 cup water.
1-4 teaspoonful cream tartar.
1 teaspoonful vanilla.
2 tablespoonfuls cream.
1-4 pound chopped almonds.
White 1 egg.

Stir together sugar, cream tartar and cold water. Cook without stirring until it threads off a fork. Beat white of egg frothy, add syrup slowly, beating; when right to spread, add cream and vanilla, spread a layer of frosting, sprinkle with chopped blanched almonds, a layer of frosting, second cake, frost, almonds on top.

BAKER'S EXTRACTS

Are the highest perfection attainable in this line. The product of this brand is the secret of many dainty desserts which so delight the epicure.

Dou You Need

a Servant of any kin , Nurse or Nurse Girl? Farmhands, Hotel Help of all kinds furnished at short notice. Personal attention given to selection of good servants. We send out nothing but good, reliable help.

Standard Employment Office,

14 MAPLE STREET.

Branch Office, 411 Main Street, Room 5.

Telephone Connections in both places.

MRS. M. C. MULVEY,

14 MAPLE STREET.

KESSELL'S
MILLINERY PARLORS

is the place to secure the Very Newest Styles in

Hats and Bonnets

——FOR——

Spring and Summer Wear.

571 MAIN STREET,

Up One Flight.   SCOTT'S BLOCK

E. T. SMITH & CO.'S SPICES, in Tin Boxes

are used and recommended by Mrs. C. E. Humphrey, Teacher of Cooking School.

NEW YORK GINGERBREAD

2 cups sugar (molasses).
1 cup butter.
4 eggs.
2 cups milk.
2 teaspoonfuls ginger.

3 tablespoonfuls baking powder (or sour milk and 1 teaspoonful soda).
6 cups flour
1-2 teaspoonful salt.

Cream butter, and sugar, add well beaten yolks of eggs and molasses (sugar); sift dry ingredients, lastly add well beaten whites of eggs. This rule makes two loaves.

HURMETS.

1 1-2 cup sugar.
2-3 cup butter.
1 cup currants.
2 eggs.
1 tablespoonful cinnamon.

1 tablespoonful nutmeg.
2 tablespoonfuls milk.
1-4 teaspoonful salt.
2 teaspoonfuls baking powder.
4 or more cups flour.

Cream butter, add sugar, eggs, mix salt, spice and baking powder to one cup flour, sift thoroughly together, add milk, and lastly floured currants, mix very stiff. Roll and cut in fancy shapes or roll bits of dough in hands and flatten in the tin by pressing each with the bottom of pint cup floured.

AMBROSIA.

4 bananas.
6 oranges.
1 pineapple.

1-2 lb. sugar.
1 cup water.

Slice the bananas, cut the orange in bits or scoop out for orange baskets, grate the pineapple. Make a syrup of the sugar and boiling water, pour over the fruit and set to cool; when cool put on the ice.

Baker's Extracts are used exclusively by the United States Government in the National Homes.

Royal Worcester Corsets.

The Shrewd Purchaser

insists on having

Royal Worcester Corsets.

They are made in so many styles that every lady can find JUST THE ONE suited to her form, and at the price she wants to pay.

OUR RETAIL STORE is Headquarters for Corsets.
Our assortment is unsurpassed.
Popular lengths and colors. The latest and most perfect models.
You can have your corsets fitted, no extra charge for trying on.
Custom work carefully attended to.
We guarantee satisfaction.
Ladies' Specialties in stock at all times.
Lady attendants.

WORCESTER CORSET COMPANY,

Retail Store, 328 Main St., Worcester, Mass.

E. T. SMITH & CO.'S SPICES, in Tin Boxes,
are used and recommended by Mrs. C. E. Humphrey, Teacher of Cooking School.

IRISH MOSS JELLY.

1-2 cup moss, 4 figs, 1 pint boiling water, 1 lemon,
1-3 cup sugar.

Wash moss, pare thinly the rind of lemon, cut figs very small. Place all these in boiling water until moss is nearly dissolved, add sugar and lemon juice. Strain into a cold, wet mold. Use an earthen mold for anything with lemon flavoring.

LEMONADE.

4 lemons, juice and rind. 1 pint boiling water.
1 2-lb lump sugar. 2 pints cold (or 3 pints hot).

Rub the lumps over the rind of lemons to extract the oil, press out juice, add boiling water, cool and put in ice box; serve with cracked ice.

FROZEN APRICOTS.

1 can apricots. 1 quart water.
1 pint sugar. 1 pint whipped cream.

Cut the apricots fine, dissolve the sugar in the water. Freeze until the consistency of mush, add the cream by folding in after the dasher is removed.

ORANGE CREAM.

3 oranges. 1-2 cup hot water.
1-2 lemon. 8 tablespoonfuls of whipped
1-2 oz. gelatine. cream.
1-2 cup cold water. Powdered sugar to taste.

Soak one-half ounce gelatine in cold water, dissolve in hot water enough to make a pint of liquid with the orange and lemon. Beat until the gelatine is dissolved, strain, stir while cooling to consitency of thick cream, add powdered sugar and eight tablespoonfuls whipped cream, beat well together. Pour into mold and set in ice to form.

Mrs. Bowen's School of Elocution and Delsarte,
34 FRONT ST., WORCESTER, MASS.

GEO. S. HOPPIN & CO.,

WHOLESALE DEALERS IN

Flour and Grain, Hay and Straw.

Sole Agents for WASHBURN, CROSBY & CO.'S Flour Mills

24 MECHANIC ST.,

WORCESTER, - MASS.

J. W. GREENE,
PLUMBER,

DEALER IN

Stoves, Ranges and Furnaces.

STEAM AND GAS FITTING.

Jobbing in all its branches promptly attended to.

51 MAIN STREET,

Cumming's Block, WORCESTER, MASS.

Telephone Connection.

E. T. SMITH & CO.'S SPICES, in Tin Boxes, are used and recommended by Mrs. C. E. Humphrey, Teacher of Cooking School.

DERBYSHIRE BREAD.

Beat three eggs until very, very light, put three pounds of flour and three ounces of butter into the larger vessel, work backward and forward until the flour is thoroughly greased and mixed with the butter. Scald one pint of milk and stand aside until lukewarm; dissolve half yeast cake in a half cup of lukewarm water; add it to the milk; then add this to the butter and flour, and beat thoroughly; add the eggs and a teaspoonful of salt; thoroughly mix the eggs with the batter, form the dough at once into small biscuits; add sufficient flour to prevent sticking; place them in a greased baking pan; cover and stand in a warm place until very light—about one and a half hours; then bake about twenty minutes in a moderate quick oven. When done, place them in a bread box until next day. Then next day dip the biscuits quickly in milk, place them in pans and stand them in a moderate oven for twenty minutes. Serve hot.

EGG BISCUIT.

Put one quart of sifted flour into the bucket; add five tablespoonfuls of sugar, a teaspoonful of baking powder, and five ounces of butter. The butter thoroughly blend with the flour. Put five eggs without separating, into the glass, and beat until very light; now add them to the flour, and beat and work until light and elastic. Cover the dough with a damp towel, and stand aside for fifteen minutes; then roll into a sheet a quarter of an inch thick; cut with a small, round cutter. Drop a few at a time into boiling water until the edges curl, then throw them into a pan of cold water for a minute; then place in greased pans and bake in a moderate oven until a light brown.

Every component part employed in producing **Baker's Extracts** is strictly pure, and the best quality obtainable

DRESSMAKING

MISS EMMA A. COLE,

Successor to
MRS. GEO. D. DAVIS,

Ladies' and Children's Dressmaking.

19 HIGH STREET,
WORCESTER, - MASS.

WM. HYLAND & SON,

Manufacturers and Dealers in

MATTRESSES,

FEATHERS, CURLED HAIR, PALMLEAF,
Husks, Excelsior, Batting and Comforters.

FEATHERS RENOVATED BY STEAM.

168 MAIN STREET,
WORCESTER, - MASS.

E. T. SMITH & CO.'S SPICES, in Tin Boxes,

are used and recommended by Mrs. C. E. Humphrey, Teacher of Cooking School.

SPICE CAKE.

1 1-4 cups sugar.
1-2 cup butter.
2 eggs.
10 raisins.
1 cup milk.
3 teaspoonfuls baking powder.
1 teaspoonful nutmeg.

1 teaspoonful cinnamon.
1 teaspoonful allspice.
1 teaspoonful ginger.
1 teaspoonful cloves.
2 1-2 cups flour measured before sifting.

Cream butter, add sugar, sift dry ingredients together. Separate eggs, add yolks to sugar, add milk and dry material, alternately, add chopped raisins rolled in flour, cut in stiffly beaten whites; bake in two small loaves.

BOILED FROSTING.

1 cup powdered sugar.
1-2 cup water.

Whites of 2 eggs.
1 teaspoonful milk.

Boil sugar and water until it threads; beat the whites frothy, add syrup, gradually beating all the while as it sets in a pan of cold water, add milk and vanilla when right to spread and put on at once.

SPONGE CAKE.

1 cup flour.
1 cup powdered sugar.
5 eggs.

Juice and rind of a lemon.
1-2 teaspoonful salt.

Separate eggs, beat the sugar into the yolks, add salt and flour gradually, the lemon juice cut in the stiff whites. Bake in a deep, papered tin, one hour in a moderate oven. Sift flour and sugar before measuring.

REAL ESTATE, Houses, Farms and House Lots For Sale and Exchange
WILLIAM GARBUTT & CO., 115 Walker Building.

FRED. W. WELLINGTON & CO.

WORCESTER, MASS.

GENERAL OFFICE,

416 MAIN STREET,

BRANCH OFFICE,

4 AUSTIN STREET,

Retail Yard, SOUTHBRIDGE ST., COR. HAMMOND ST.

E. T. SMITH & CO.'S SPICES, in Tin Boxes,
are used and recommended by Mrs. C. E. Humphrey, Teacher of Cooking School.

POTATOES AU GRATIN.

1 pint potato balls.   1 cup prepared bread crumbs.
1 cup thin white sauce.

Cut potatoes into small balls, cook ten minutes in salted water, season with salt, pepper and celery salt. Butter an earthen baking dish, put in the potato and pour on the white sauce, cover with the crumbs, brown in a quick oven.

SAUCE.—Two tablespoonfuls butter, melted, stir in a level tablespoonful flour and one cup hot milk, salt and pepper.

SCALLOPED POTATOES.

1 pint cold cubed potatoes.   1-3 cup butter.
1 cup white sauce.   1-2 teaspoonful salt.
1 cup cracker crumbs.   1-4 teaspoonful pepper.

Place in an earthen dish, half the potato and half the white sauce, the rest of the potato and sauce. Prepare the cracker crumbs by rolling in melted butter thoroughly and place over the whole.

POTATO BALLS.

12 large potatoes.   White pepper.
1 tablespoonful lemon juice.   Salt.
3 tablespoons chopped parsley

Cut the balls with a vegetable scoop into a dish of cold water, cook 12 minutes in salted boiling water, drain and dry by shaking in pan over the range. Mix parsley, lemon juice and salt and pepper, add to to the melted butter. Pour over the balls and serve in a hot dish.

Baker's Non-Alcoholic Ginger, An unfailing remedy for Colds, Cramps, Colic, Chills, Diarrhœa, and all forms of Summer Complaint.

GATELY & ROGERS Furniture Company,

282 MAIN ST.,

Opp. Bay State House, Worcester, Mass.

WE FURNISH YOUR HOUSE WITH

Chamber Sets, Iron Beds, Mattresses, Pillows, Parlor Sets, Extension Tables, Sideboards, China Closets, Buffet Tables, all kinds of Chairs, Bed Lounges, Lounges, Couches, Parlor Stoves, Oil Stoves, and the Famous Oakland Ranges, Oil Cloth, Straw Matting, Carpets, Refrigerators and Baby Carriages.

On Easy Payments if wanted.

STEARNS' CRACKERS

ARE BEST.

There are imitations of course, but you want the best. Insist upon having them of your Grocer.

ROGERS'
Bread and Cracker Works.

E. T. SMITH & CO.'S SPICES in Tin Boxes,

are used and recommended by Mrs. C. E. Humphrey, Teacher of Cooking School.

CHEESE BISCUIT.

Grate a half cup of cheese, mix with six hard boiled eggs chopped fine; add 1 a tablespoonful of French mustard, a half teaspoonful of salt and a saltspoonful of pepper; rub these well together; then add two tablespoonfuls of melted butter; then spread this mixture, thinly, on small, round water crackers, "hard tack."

HOMINY MUFFINS.

Two cupfuls of boiled hominy; beat it smooth; stir in three cupfuls sour milk, half cup melted butter, two teaspoonfuls of salt, two tablespoonfuls sugar; add three eggs well beaten, one teaspoonful soda, dissolved in hot water; two cupfuls flour. Bake quickly.

MUFFINS.

A tablespoonful of melted butter and two well beaten eggs may be added to the bread sponge, and if stood aside for two hours and baked in gem pans, makes a most delicious muffin.

HYGENIC BUNS.

Bread to be perfectly healthful should be light, yet entirely free from baking powder or other chemical substance. The great labor involved in beating batters and dough light has rendered the use of baking powder almost universal.

One pint of water, 1 1-2 pints flour, three eggs, teaspoonful of salt, and one tablespoonful melted butter. Beat the water and flour together until light, add salt and butter. Beat the whites of the eggs stiff, then add to them the yolks and beat until light; add these to the batter and stir in with as little beating as possible.

Those who prefer can add one teaspoonful of baking powder to the mixture. Bake thirty minutes in a quick oven.

WILLIAM GARBUTT & CO., Real Estate and Loan Agency
115 WALKER BUILDING. Open Evenings.

C. E. MINCKLER,

Dealer in a Full Line of

Fine Groceries and Meats.

YOUR ORDERS KINDLY SOLICITED.

Orders taken at the House if desired.

16 Woodland St.,   WORCESTER, MASS.

Telephone 181-4.

MRS. F. E. MORGAN,

52 PLEASANT STREET,   WORCESTER, MASS.

Bread and Rolls.

Rolls baked to order for Church Sociables, Weddings, Dinners, Suppers, etc., on short notice.

ENTIRE WHEAT BREAD.

E. T. SMITH & CO.'S SPICES, in Tin Boxes

are used and recommended by Mrs. C. E. Humphrey, Teacher of Cooking School.

ANGEL CAKE.

Four ounces flour, 12 eggs (whites only), three fourths pound sugar (granulated), one teaspoonful vanilla extract. First sift the flour and cream tartar together five or six times. Line a deep, square cake pan with paper; do not grease it. Beat the whites of the eggs VERY STIFF. Then gradually add the sugar. Continue beating until perfectly smooth. Flavor this with the vanilla. Now add the flour quickly. Put in the oven immediately, and bake forty five minutes.

A FINE FRUIT CAKE.

Twelve ounces flour, twelve ounces butter, twelve ounces sugar, ten eggs, one teaspoonful grated nutmeg, one-half teaspoonful grated mace, three fourths pound raisins, three-fourths pound currants, four ounces citron, four ounces candied lemon, one wine glass brandy.

Sift the flour, grate the nutmeg, seed the raisins, and chop together with the citron and the lemon. Wash the currants and sift through a coarse sieve with a little flour. This will receive loose stems, etc. Cream the butter and sugar, then add the eggs, beating until light and smooth. Now add the chopped fruit and currants. Mix. Put the nutmeg and mace into the brandy, and pour over the whole mixture. Mix thoroughly and bake two and a half hours in a moderate oven.

Baker's Preparations Are used by the leading Hotels, Restaurants and thousands of Families, all of whom speak in the highest terms of their superior qualities.

Dress and Cloak Making.

Rooms 19 and 20 Knowles Building,

518 MAIN STREET,

WORCESTER, - MASS.

Ladies' Hair Emporium

ARTISTIC WORK IN
Wigs, Switches, Frizzes, Etc.

HAIR DRESSING IN LATEST STYLES.

SCALP TREATED IN VERY BEST MANNER.

Only Ladies in attendance.

MISS I. F. BOND,

571 MAIN STREET.

E. T. SMITH & CO.'S SPICES, in Tin Boxes,
are used and recommended by Mrs. C E. Humphrey, Teacher of Cooking School.

SOUTHERN GOLD LOAF.

Pare and boil six medium-sized potatoes. When done drain, press through a colander, and add one large tablespoonful of lard or butter, one tablespoonful of sugar, and six eggs, well beaten. Beat the whole continuously for two minutes; add a half pint milk and a pint of flour; beat again, and when lukewarm add a teacupful of yeast. Mix and stand in a moderately warm place over night. Early in the morning add sufficient flour to make a soft dough. Knead and work thoroughly until the dough will not stick to the hands or board. Form into small loaves; place in greased pans, and when very light bake in a moderately quick oven about forty minutes. Serve warm.

CORNMEAL WAFFLES.

Put a pint of boiling water into a saucepan and stir into it sufficient dry cornmeal (about two-thirds of a cup) to make a mush. Lift the cornmeal in your left hand; allow it to pass slowly between the fingers into the water, while you stir quickly with the right hand. Let the mush cook slowly for twenty minutes; then add two ounces of butter and a dessert spoonful of salt, and stand aside to cool. When cold separate four eggs, add the yolks to the mush; then add half a pint of buttermilk or sour cream. Now stir in gradually sufficient flour, about one pint, to make a thinnish batter. Dissolve a half teaspoonful of bi-carbonate of soda in a tablespoonful of boiling water, and add it to the batter. Stir in quickly the well-beaten whites of eggs and they are ready to bake.

Baker's Extracts Are double the strength of ordinary extracts, which makes them the most economical to use.

ALL GOOD COOKS

—— WANT ——

Good Pictures AT Reasonable Prices.

THE PLACE FOR SUCH WORK IS AT

Hevy

Crayon Artist and Photographer.

397 MAIN STREET,

Cor. Mechanic,   WORCESTER.

E. T. SMITH & CO.'S SPICES, in Tin Boxes

are used and recommended by Mrs. C. E. Humphrey, Teacher of Cooking School.

WATER WAFERS.

Put one quart of sifted flour into a vessel; add a quarter pound of butter and a tablespoonful salt; mix gently until the butter has thoroughly disappeared; add gradually sufficiently cold water to moisten the flour. Now turn the beater slowly and continuously for five minutes, or until the dough is smooth and elastic; take it out on a board, mould it lightly, roll out as thin as a wafer, cut into small, round cakes, stick with a fork here and there over the surface and bake in a moderately quick oven, until a light brown, about five minutes.

BERWICK SPONGE CAKE.

Beat six eggs without separating, and nine ounces granulated sugar until light and creamy. Weigh twelve ounces flour; sift one-half lightly into the eggs and sugar, mixing it in carefully. Dissolve two even teaspoonfuls cream of tartar into a gill of water; add this to the cake; beat one minute; then add the remaining flour, the juice and grated rind of one lemon, and a quarter teaspoonful salt, mix thoroughly, and add a level teaspoonful soda dissolved in four tablespoonfuls hot water; beat the whole to a light, smooth mass, and bake in long square pans in a quick oven.

POP OVERS.

Two eggs, one cup milk, one cup flour, one teaspoonful salt. Beat the eggs very little, just sufficient to mix, then add milk and salt, and then the flour; mix until smooth and put into the hot, greased iron pans. Bake in a quick oven twenty minutes.

Baker's Extracts have many imitators, but no equals. One trial proves their worth.

WORCESTER
School of Oratory and Music
492 MAIN ST., WORCESTER, MASS.

*Newest, Best and Most Approved Methods.
Experienced Teachers. Lowest Prices.*

A Systematic Course of Instruction in Reading, Oratory, Dramatic, Lyric and Pantomimic Art. A thorough system of Gesture.

MUSIC :—Voice, Piano and Violin. New England Conservatory methods. Same instruction given as in the large schools of Boston and at a much more moderate cost.

SEND FOR CIRCULAR.

MISS STELLA M. HAYNES, Principal.

Metropolitan Storage Warerooms.
FURNITURE MOVING.
Household Furniture, Pianos and Merchandise
STORED IN SAFE AND CLEAN APARTMENTS.

Packing Furniture and other Goods for Families Moving will receive Particular Attention.

6 BARTON PLACE,
WORCESTER, - *MASS.*

Telephone 646-3.

E. T. SMITH & CO.'S SPICES in Tin Boxes, are used and recommended by Mrs. C. E. Humphrey, Teacher of Cooking School.

BREAD CAKE.

When the bread sponge is light and ready to mould put aside one pint of the dough. Put this dough into the bucket; add three ounces butter, one cup sugar, two eggs, and the rind of half a lemon, grated. Now beat until the ingredients are thoroughly mixed; then continue until the mixture is light. Now add carefully one cup currants that have been washed, dried, and thoroughly floured. Mix them gently, and pour the cake into a greased pan to the depth of one inch. Put four tablespoonfuls brown sugar, two ounces butter, one tablespoonful flour and a teaspoonful sugar into the glass, and beat until light; then add and stir in gently two heaping tablespoonfuls stale bread crumbs; put this mixture here and there over the top of the cake, pressing it down with the finger; stand in a warm place to rise, and when light bake in a moderately quick oven, protecting the top that it may not get too brown

CREAM CAKE.

Six ounces flour, four ounces butter, nine ounces sugar, eight eggs, one teaspoonful vanilla. Sift the flour THREE times. Beat the butter and sugar to a cream, to this add the eggs, and beat until VERY LIGHT, add the vanilla, lastly the flour. Bake in jelly pans forty minutes.

For the cream: One and one-half pints sweet milk, four eggs, YOLKS only, one tablespoonful corn starch, sufficient sifted flour to thicken, one teaspoonful rose water. Put the corn starch and milk in the vessel together, mix them, add sufficient sifted flour to thicken to the consistency of custard. Beat yolks until VERY LIGHT and add to the custard; pour the whole in a double boiler and cook, STIRRING until it thickens; when nearly done add the rose water.

HOUSEKEEPERS

run no risk in using BAKER'S EXTRACTS. They are of unvarying quality.

C. C. LOWELL,

DEALER IN

Paints, Oils, Glass, Brushes, Etc.

ALSO MATHEMATICAL SUPPLIES AND

ARTISTS' GOODS.

White China and Materials for Decorating same.

12 PEARL STREET, WORCESTER.

E. T. SMITH & CO.'S PICES, in Tin Boxes,

are used and recommended by Mrs. C. E. Humphrey, Teacher of Cooking School.

VIRGINIA WAFERS.

Powder two ounces lard into one quart flour; add a teaspoonful salt, and stir in gradually sufficient milk, about a half pint, to make a soft dough. Work and knead this dough CONTINUOUSLY for fifteen minutes. It must be soft and full of blisters. Pull off a piece about the size of a small egg, and roll it out into a cake about six or seven inches in diameter and as thin as a wafer; stick regularly over the top with a fork, place on lightly greased pie tins and bake in a very moderate oven until thoroughly done, without browning. These wafer like biscuits are exceedingly nice to serve with cheese or preserves.

MILK BISCUIT.

Put one quart flour into a vessel; add a large tablespoonful, or two ounces butter, and a teaspoonful salt; work backward and forward an instant, mix with the butter; then add two heaping teaspoonfuls of baking powder, and sufficient milk, about ha'f a pint to make a soft dough. Mix quickly, take out on a board and roll about one inch in thickness. Cut with a small, round cutter, and bake in a quick oven fifteen minutes. Do not allow the biscuits to touch each other while baking. These biscuits can be made in five minutes and are delightful.

BAKESTONE CAKES.

Rub one ounce butter into one quart flour, until the flour is well greased; add a teaspoonful salt and sufficient thin cream to moisten, beating vigorously all the while. A dough, not a batter, must be formed. Work the dough for just one minute; roll it out half an inch thick; cut with a biscuit cutter, and bake quickly on a hot griddle.

Baker's Extracts, whether used in the substantial dishes or dainty desserts, will be found equally satisfactory.

Grand Central Market,

FRONT STREET,

WORCESTER, MASS.

CARRIE FRANCES RICE,
9 High Street.

Manicure.
Chiropodist.

Every lady should have her Nails Cultivated and Beautified.

Corns Removed, 25 cents each also Ingrowing Nails and Bunions treated.

A Superior and Complete line of Toilet Articles.

Millinery Parlors.

MRS. H. A. GREEN,
9 HIGH STREET.

Exclusive Designs.

Choice Goods.

Prices Reasonable

E. T. SMITH & CO.'S SPICES, in Tin Boxes, are used and recommended by Mrs. C. E. Humphrey, Teacher of Cooking School.

TEA BISCUIT.

One quart flour, four heaping teaspoonfuls baking powder, half teaspoonful salt, two tablespoonfuls butter. Whip these two together until they are thorougly POWDERED, then add one pint milk and mix properly. The dough should be just stiff enough to roll out. Cut and place in buttered pans; bake about twenty minutes in a quick oven. These biscuit surpass any we have ever seen.

CORN BREAD.

Beat together rapidly, from one to five minutes, the following ingredients: two heaping cups cornmeal, one cup flour, two and a half cups milk, one teaspoonful lard, two of white sugar, one of soda, two of cream tartar and one of salt. Beat three eggs light and stir in gently. Bake quickly and steadily in a buttered mold.

TEA CAKE.

One pound flour, one teaspoonful butter, one teaspoonful lard, sweet milk, one teaspoonful soda, two teaspoonfuls cream tartar. Sift soda, cream tartar and flour together, mix thoroughly with the butter and lard. To this add sufficient sweet milk to make a dough. Roll to the thickness of half an inch, cut into three cornered pieces and bake twenty minutes in a moderate oven. Butter and serve hot.

FINE GINGER SNAPS.

One pint molasses, one pound sugar, twelve ounces butter, one ounce lemon peel, one ounce ground ginger, one teaspoonful soda, flour sifted. Chop the lemon peel; sift the flour. Beat to a cream the butter and sugar. Add the molasses and mix thoroughly, then the lemon peel and ground ginger. Now sift in the flour and soda, flour sufficient to make a stiff dough. Cut in form and bake in a quick, hot oven.

DIVORCE AND PROBATE BUSINESS A SPECIALTY.

ADAMS FRANKLIN BROWN, Attorney, Room 201 Walker Building, 405 Main St., Worcester.

GEO. M. WOODWARD,

Attorney and Counsellor at Law

ROOM 16, WALKER BUILDING,

405 MAIN ST.,   **WORCESTER, MASS.**

GEORGE L. BARR,

Manufacturer and Dealer in Extra Quality

Trunks, Traveling Bags,

AND FANCY LEATHER GOODS.

Sample Trunks made to order.   Prices always the lowest.

14 FRONT ST., WORCESTER, MASS.

L. W. PENNINGTON,

Designer, Manufacturing Jeweler

AND DIAMOND SETTER.

BADGES AND EMBLEMS MADE TO ORDER.

Gilding, Acid Coloring and Oxidizing, Repairing, Etc.
Old Gold and Silver Purchased.

ALSO MANUFACTURER OF ELECTRIC PENCIL.

397 MAIN ST.,   COR MECHANIC ST.,

WORCESTER, MASS.

I. L. CURRIER, REAL ESTATE AND MORTGAGE LOANS,
405 MAIN ST., WORCESTER, MASS.

DUTCH APPLE CAKE.

One pint pastry flour, one-half teaspoonful salt, 2 teaspoonfuls baking powder, one-half cup butter, one egg, one cup milk, two tablespoonfuls sugar, sour apples. Mix flour, salt and baking powder, add well beaten egg and melted butter, stir thoroughly, adding milk gradually, then beat. Cut the apples into rather thick slices and arrange in two rows, pressing in. Bake about twenty five minutes in a quick oven. Sprinkle with granulated sugar before baking. Serve with lemon sauce.

BREAD.

One cup hot milk, one cup cold water, one tablespoonful shortening, one tablespoonful sugar, one teaspoonful salt, one-fourth yeast cake, dissolved in a half cup lukewarm water, six or seven cups bread flour. Put into a bowl the sugar, salt, and shortening, pour on the hot milk and stir till dissolved, then add the cup cold water, and the yeast dissolved in the lukewarm water; stir in five cups flour and gradually add enough more to make it stiff enough to knead. Cover; let it rise till it has doubled its bulk, then cut it down and shape it into loaves and biscuit. Let it rise again in the pans, and bake forty or fifty minutes.

QUAKER BISCUIT.

Scald one cup Quaker Rolled Oats with one pint boiling water, and let it stand one hour. Add a half teaspoonful shortening, a scant half cup molasses, half teaspoonful salt, half yeast cake disso ved in one-third cup lukewarm water and five cups sifted bread flour. Let it rise and when it has doubled its bulk shape into small biscuit. Let them rise till double, then bake in a hot oven twenty minutes.

This makes three dozen biscuit.

DIVORCE AND PROBATE BUSINESS a Specialty.
ADAMS FRANKLIN BROWN, Attorney, Room 201 Walker building, 405 Main St., Worcester.

Standard Laundry,

HAAS BROS., Props.

58 SOUTHBRIDGE ST., WORCESTER, MASS.

ALL WORK DONE BY HAND.

First Class Work at Moderate Prices. Goods called for and delivered in all parts of the city.

The Virgil Practice Clavier,
A TONELESS INSTRUMENT FOR TEACHING AND PRACTICE.

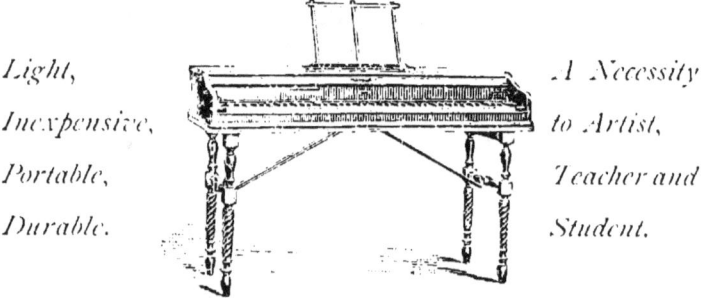

Light,
Inexpensive,
Portable,
Durable.

A Necessity
to Artist,
Teacher and
Student.

The effect from the use of the Clavier is to make the touch accurate, firm, vigorous, elastic, sensitive, discriminative, delicate, enduring and finished. It stops annoyance from piano practice, saves a good piano, and, rightly used, secures greater artistic playing skill in one year than can be acquired at the piano in three years, and frequently greater than is EVER gotten at the piano.

H. S. WILDER, Sole Representative for Eastern Massachusetts.

160 BOYLSTON ST., BOSTON.   518 MAIN ST., WORCESTER

BARGAINS IN REAL ESTATE ALWAYS ON HAND AT
I. L. CURRIER'S, 405 MAIN STREET, WORCESTER, MASS.

SNOW COCOANUT CAKE.

Eight ounces sugar, half cup butter, twelve ounces flour, eight eggs, WHITES only, half cup milk, one teaspoonful vanilla, fourth teaspoonful soda, half teaspoonful cream tartar, one teaspoonful rose water. Cream the butter and sugar, add the whites of eggs and beat well; to this add the milk and vanilla; mix. Sift the flour, soda and cream tartar and add these to the mixture. Bake in jelly pans. Take grated cocoanut and mix with a little powdered sugar, slightly dampened; let this dry and then make alternate layers of the cake and cocoanut. Frost the top, flavor with the rose water.

The above is considered a delicious morsel.

WHITE FRUIT CAKE.

One pound flour, one pound butter, one and a fourth pound sugar, fourteen eggs, two pounds citron, one pound candied orange, one and a half pound dessicated cocoanut, two pounds almonds, one wine glass brandy, one wine glass sherry, two teaspoonfuls mace, two teaspoonfuls cinnamon, one teaspoonful grated nutmeg, two teaspoonfuls vanilla.

Sift the flour, chop the orange, citron and almonds with the chopper (having previously blanched the almonds), cream the butter and sugar, to this add the WHITES OF ALL the eggs and four yolks; beat until very light, now add all the fruit with the mace, cinnamon and nutmeg; when this is thoroughly mixed put in the vanilla, brandy and sherry; mix again, lastly add the flour, mix very thoroughly with a back and forward stroke. Cover top with paper, bake two hours.

SCOURING AND SWIMMING BATHS COMBINED at JENSEN'S Turkish and Russian Bath Establishment for Ladies and Gentlemen.
No. 1 SUDBURY STREET. Opposite Bay State House

G. T. LINDFORS,
ENGRAVER

398 MAIN ST., WORCESTER, MASS.

Lettering on Silverware, Fine Inscriptions, Monograms and Cyphers
DONE WITH SPECIAL CARE.

DOOR PLATES (only best quality Silver Plates) a Specialty. Orders received for Wedding and Visiting Cards.

ESTABLISHED 1877.

J. T. CAHILL,

Practical Plumber and Sanitary Engineer.

GAS FITTING, STEAM AND HOT WATER HEATING.

18 PLEASANT STREET,
WORCESTER, - MASS.
Telephone 87-3.

BARGAINS IN REAL ESTATE ALWAYS ON HAND AT
J. L. CURRIER, 405 Main Street, Worcester.

GINGER SNAPS (plain).

One cup brown sugar, one cup butter, one cup lard, two cups molasses, half cup milk, two tablespoonfuls ground ginger, half tablespoonful soda, 1 tablespoonful cream tartar. Beat the lard, butter and sugar to a cream, add the molasses, mix, then the milk and ginger, mix well; now sift the soda and cream tartar with the flour, add sufficient flour to make a light dough. Roll thin, cut in forms. Bake.

JELLY CAKE.

One pound sugar, one and a half pound flour, three-fourths pound butter, nine eggs, one-fourth teaspoonful soda, one-half teaspoonful cream tartar. Put the sugar and butter in the vessel and beat until perfectly creamed; now add the eggs and beat until smooth and thick. Sift the flour with the soda and cream tartar, and add the mixture with a slow back and forward stroke.

FRENCH RUSK.

Scald one pint milk and add one-fourth cup sugar, two tablespoonfuls butter, one and a half teaspoonfuls salt; when lukewarm add one-third yeast cake dissolved in one-fourth cup water and add three cups flour; let it rise until it doubles its bulk. Add one egg and two yolks beaten well, and enough flour to knead; let it rise again, shape, put into pan and brush over with the white of an egg slightly beaten, to which has been added a tablespoonful sugar, one-half tablespoonful water and a few drops vanilla. Bake in a hot oven twenty minutes.

FOR TURKISH AND RUSSIAN BATHS, go to JENSEN'S ESTABLISHMENT
for Ladies and Gentlemen at No. 1 Sudbury St., opp. Bay State House.

E. B. GOODSPEED,
Furniture Finishing, Painting and Repairing.
Pianos Polished, Organs Refinished, French Polishing, Pictures Framed, Gilding and Bronzing.

38 CENTRAL STREET, - - WORCESTER, MASS.

J. C. WARREN,
DEALER IN
Wood and Kindlings.
Orders Promptly Attended to. Postal Cards furnished.

46 UNION ST., Residence, 12 ELLIOTT ST.

WORCESTER, MASS.

L. J. ZAHONYI,
Confectioner and Caterer.

Weddings, Parties, Suppers, etc., supplied on short notice and reasonable terms.

ICE CREAM WHOLESALE AND RETAIL.

21 PLEASANT STREET,
Lothrop's Opera House building.

BARGAINS IN REAL ESTATE ALWAYS ON HAND AT
J. L. CURRIER, 405 Main Street, Worcester.

CREAM OF HALIBUT SOUP.

Cook one pound halibut in boiling, salted water twenty minutes, or until the flesh leaves the bones. Drain and rub through a sieve; scald one quart milk with a slice of onion and blade mace; then remove the onion and mace and add the milk gradually to the fish and thicken with a tablespoonful each of butter and flour, cooked together. Remove from the fire, add a tablespoonful of butter in bits; pour into a tureen, sprinkling with finely cut parsley.

SPRING SOUP.

Cook two or three large Bermuda onions, sliced thin, in one tablespoonful butter, fifteen minutes, not browning them as it is a white soup. Add them to two quarts white stock made from veal, also half small loaf bakers bread which has been broken into small pieces. Simmer two hours, then rub through a sieve and add a quart of milk. Melt two tablespoonfuls butter, add two rounding tablespoonfuls flour, and combine with the soup. Season with salt and pepper, and serve with toasted bread.

BAKED BEAN SOUP.

To three cups baked beans add three pints water, two slices onion and two stalks celery. Simmer thirty minutes and rub through a sieve. Add to this one and a half cup stewed and strained tomatoes, half tablespoonful chile sauce, and salt and pepper to taste. Put into a saucepan one tablespoonful butter, and when it melts add a tablespoonful flour, mix well and stir into the soup. Cook two or three minutes and serve with toasted crackers.

TUB BATHS at JENSEN'S Turkish and Russian Bath Establishment for Ladies and Gentlemen.
1 Sudbury St., opp. Bay State House. Telephone connection.

 **Rubber Stamps** for Linen, Paper, Wood &c

Silver, Nickel and Aluminum **DOOR PLATES.**

Metal Stamps of all kinds.

Marking Ink and Fountains

FROST'S STAMP AND INK WORKS,
535 MAIN STREET. OPPOSITE CHATHAM

RICHARD J. HEALEY,
371 AND 373 MAIN STREET.

HEADQUARTERS FOR

Fine Shoes of Every Description.

Acme Plating Works,
13 MECHANIC STREET, ROOM 16,
WORCESTER, MASS.
J. N. MASSICOTT, Proprietor.

ELECTROPLATING
Gold, Silver, Nickel, Copper, Brass, Aluminum.

Polishing, Buffing, Bronzing, Oxidizing, Coloring, Lacquering, Etc.

USE B. M. C. BEST FLOUR. It is absolute perfection, and most economical for family use.
FOR SALE BY ALL GROCERS.

ZEPHYR ROLLS.

One quart sifted pastry flour, one even teaspoonful salt, three rounding teaspoonfuls baking powder, one large tablespoonful butter, milk to make a soft dough, one egg; add baking powder and salt to the flour and sift twice. Rub in the butter with the fingers, till there are no large lumps. Beat the egg till light and add it to the milk; mix in the milk and egg gradually, using a broad knife and wetting only a part of the flour with each addition of milk and egg; when just stiff enough to be handled (not kneaded) turn out onto a well floured board, pat it out with a rolling pin till half an inch thick, then cut it into rounds, fold over. Bake about fifteen minutes in a hot oven.

CREAM MUFFINS.

One pint pastry flour, half teaspoonful salt, two teaspoonfuls baking powder, yolks two eggs beaten till thick, one-fourth cup cream, or enough to make a drop batter, whites two eggs beaten stiff. Bake in muffin pan and serve hot.

TEA CAKES.

Two cups pastry flour, two teaspoonfuls baking powder, one-fourth cup sugar, half teaspoonful salt, one egg, one cup milk, one tablespoonful butter, melted. Mix in the order given and bake in gem pans or cups in a hot oven about twenty minutes.

INDIAN CAKE.

One cup granulated corn meal, one-half cup pastry flour, one fourth cup sugar, two teaspoonfuls baking powder, one tablespoonful butter, melted, half teaspoonful salt, one egg, one cup milk. Put all the dry things into the mixing bowl, add melted butter; beat egg till light, mix it with the milk; then add it to the dry things, beat well; pour into a shallow pan and bake in a hot oven twenty minutes.

Fine Home Made Candies

MADE BY US FRESH DAILY.

LIVINGSTON'S,
622 MAIN STREET.

P. D. BENOIT,
⇒ ARTIST ⇐

PORTRAITS in OIL, PASTEL and CRAYON
Made from Life or copied from small pictures.

When there is so much cheap work being palmed on the public, do not be duped into paying a price for a "Solar Print" Finish in Crayon that ought to insure you a Genuine "Free Hand" Portrait, Artistically Painted.

Yours sincerely, P. D. BENOIT.

STUDIO, 28 CHANDLER ST.,   WORCESTER, MASS

INSTRUCTION GIVEN.

USE B. M. C. BEST FLOUR. It is absolute perfection, and most economical for family use.
FOR SALE BY ALL GROCERS.

POTATO SOUP.

Four potatoes, one quart milk, two teaspoonfuls chopped onion, two teaspoonfuls salt, one teaspoonful celery salt, half saltspoonful white pepper, quarter saltspoon cayenne, one tablespoonful flour, two tablespoonfuls butter.

Cook the potatoes in boiling water till very soft; cook onions with the milk in a double boiler. When the potatoes are done drain off the water and mash them; add the hot milk and seasoning. Rub through a strainer and put on to boil again. Put butter in a saucepan, and when melted add flour, and when well mixed stir into the soup. Let it boil five minutes and serve very hot.

FRIED SMELTS.

Clean the smelts, dry and season with salt and pepper. Skewer into shape by putting the tail of the fish into its mouth and fastening with a small wooden skewer, or tooth pick. Dip in flour, in egg, and again in dried bread crumbs, and fry in a frying basket in deep fat. The fat should be hot enough to brown a piece of bread while you count sixty, as a clock ticks. When they are in the fat set the kettle back; cook large ones five minutes and small ones four. Drain on brown paper and serve with

SAUCE TARTAN.

One tablespoonful vinegar, one teaspoonful lemon juice, one saltspoonful salt, one tablespoonful Worcestershire sauce, one third cup butter. Mix vinegar, lemon juice, salt and sauce in a small bowl, and heat over hot water. Brown the butter in a frying pan and strain into the other mixture.

Mrs. Bowen's School of Elocution and Delsarte,
34 FRONT ST., WORCESTER, MASS.

A. L. BEMIS,
Window and Door Screens,

PATTERN AND CABINET MAKING

SATISFACTION GUARANTEED.

180 UNION STREET, — WORCESTER, MASS.

TELEPHONE 39-5.

WM. H. GATES

Counsellor at Law,

26 PEARL STREET.

MISS A. FRAZIER

Dressmaking Rooms,

NO. 1 CHATHAM STREET,
COR. MAIN ST.

First Class Work Done.
Prices Moderate.

Latest Styles Now Ready.

USE B. M. C. BEST FLOUR. It is absolute perfection, and most economical for family use.
FOR SALE BY ALL GROCERS.

DUCHESS SOUP.

Cook two slices each of carrot and onion in one tablespoonful butter three minutes and add to one quart white stock, with a blade of mace. Cook fifteen minutes, strain and add one pint milk, or part milk and part cream. Thicken with two tablespoonfuls butter and two of flour, which have been cooked together, seasoning with salt and pepper to taste. Lastly stir in four rounding tablespoonfuls grated cream cheese, then cook for two minutes and serve immediately. The milk should not be added till just before the soup is to be served.

CLAM SOUP WITH POACHED EGGS.

One quart clams, one quart fresh milk, one slice onion, three tablespoonfuls butter, one tablespoonful salt, three tablespoonfuls flour, one teaspoonful salt, half saltspoonful pepper, a light grating nutmeg, whites three eggs.

ut clams in a colander, pour over them a half cup cold water; free them from any foreign substance, cut off the black necks and separate the soft parts from the hard. Chop the hard parts, add these with the soft parts to the clam liquor, heat slowly to the boiling point, then strain through a cheese cloth and strainer. Scald the milk with the onion, melt the butter, add the flour, mix well, then add it to the boiling clam liquor; add also the hot milk from which the onion has been removed; cook for two minutes, then season with salt, pepper, and nutmeg, and just before serving pour on the beaten whites of the eggs. The whites should be beaten frothy and not stiff.

T. D. GARD, Jewelry and Repairer,
393 MAIN ST., WORCESTER, MASS.

THE WORCESTER, THE HOME, THE EQUITY,
Co-Operative Banks,

WALKER BUILDING,   405 MAIN STREET.

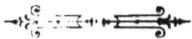

These banks help people buy houses, pay off mortgages, build homes and save money. From $1 to $75 can be invested each month by any person, and begin earning dividends at once, the lowest rate being 6 per cent. Three times a month, all money on hand is loaned at auction. These loans may be repaid at any time, but nothing can be demanded on them except the monthly payments of about $10.50 on each thousand dollars, which finally cancel the debts. The Banks are incorporated, and are under the supervision of the Massachusetts Bank Commissioners.

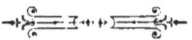

THE WORCESTER, STEPHEN C. EARLE, Pres.
    THE HOME, E. H. TOWNE, Pres.
        THE EQUITY, CHAS. L. GATES, Pres.
    THOS. J. HASTINGS, Sec'y.

TAKE YOUR JEWELRY REPAIRING TO
T. D. GARD, 393 Main St., Worcester.

SALT COD STEWED.

Cover one cup chopped codfish with cold water, and soak two hours. Pare and chop two medium sized potatoes, put them in a stewing pan, cover with boiling water and boil five minutes; drain, add one pint milk, a tablespoonful butter and add a half cup chopped stale bread. Do not forget that the Perfection chopper will chop the codfish, potatoes and bread, and it is not necessary to clean the machine until all are chopped. Drain the fish, scald it and drain again, and add it to the other ingredients; let it boil up once, add a palatable seasoning of salt and pepper, and serve very hot.

DEVILED OYSTERS.

Drain and chop twenty-five nice fat oysters, then drain again. Put a half pint of cream on to boil. Rub one rounding tablespoonful butter with two of flour, and add to the cream when boiling; stir continually until it thickens, then add the yolks of two eggs slightly beaten, cook a moment, take from the fire and add a tablespoonful chopped parsley, the oysters, salt and cayenne to taste. Have the deep shells of oysters washed perfectly clean, fill them with this mixture, sprinkle lightly with bread crumbs, stand them in a baking pan and brown in a very quick oven. Serve in the shells and garnish with parsley. A word of caution: Avoid long cooking as it makes them hard and dry.

SMOTHERED OYSTERS, OR FANCY ROAST.

Put a tablespoonful butter in a covered saucepan, with half a saltspoonful white pepper, one teaspoonful salt and a few grains cayenne. When hot add one pint oysters carefully prepared. Cover closely and shake the pan to keep the oysters from sticking; cook two or three minutes, or till plump. Serve on toasted crackers.

EKLUND'S JUNIPER BEER is a refreshing, healthful and delicious beverage. Sold everywhere and manufactured by C. A. EKLUND & CO., 5 Thomas St. and 101 Green St., Worcester, Mass.

JOHN KENDALL   DAVID BOYDEN

JOHN KENDALL & CO.
Hatters and Furriers.

We are the Oldest Hat, Cap and Fur House in the city, and are too well known to need an extended introduction. By dealing in the better class of goods, giving good value for the money, not misrepresenting articles sold, and attending to our own business, we have been enabled thus far, to live and pay our bills, and propose for a while longer to show to the people of *Worcester* and vicinity a full line of *Hats, Caps and Furs*. We make a specialty of *Furs and Fur Repairing*. Our stock will be found to be complete at all times and consists of *Furs for Ladies and Gentlemen, Coats, Caps, Gloves, Muffs, Setts and Trimming*. We always carry a large line of *Fur Robes*. Our *Work Room* is connected with our store, and we are enabled by having skilled help, to turn out the finest kind of Fur Work. A cordial invitation is extended to all readers of this to call in and look at our stock of *Hats, Caps and Furs* at

315 MAIN STREET,
JOHN KENDALL & CO.

T. D. GARD, 393 Main St., Worcester.
RINGS, BADGES, CHAINS, AND MADE TO ORDER.

LOBSTER CREAM.

One two-pound lobster, half cup bread crumbs, half cup milk, quarter cup thick cream, half teaspoonful salt, a few grains cayenne and the whites of three eggs. Remove the meat from the lobster and chop fine. Cook bread crumbs with the milk until reduced to a paste, and add the cream. Lastly add the whites of eggs beaten, add it to the lobster meat and season with the salt and pepper, and add the cream. Lastly add the whites of eggs, beaten stiff, and turn the mixture into buttered molds, covered with buttered papers, to fit the top of each. Set them in a pan of hot water and bake twenty or thirty minutes. The water should come half as high as the molds. Turn each one onto a plate, and pour around them lobster sauce. This is sufficient for eight or nine persons.

BAKED HALIBUT.

Have slices of halibut cut about three fourths inch thick, Wipe with a wet cloth; sprinkle over each slice, lemon juice, onion juice, salt and pepper. Let them stand half an hour, then spread both sides with melted butter and flour and dudge with flour. Bake twenty minutes and serve with

WHITE SAUCE.

Put into double boiler one pint milk or half milk and half white stock and one slice onion. When hot put into a saucepan two level tablespoonfuls butter, and when melted and bubbling add two rounding tablespoonfuls flour, mix well, then add the hot milk, a little at a time, stirring and beating between each addition. Season with salt and pepper. The slice of onion must be removed from the milk. To obtain onion juice rub an onion across a grater and then press till the juice begins to flow.

T. D. GARD, 393 Main St., Worcester.
SILVERSMITH AND REPAIRING OF ALL KINDS.

BOARDMAN BROS.,

Successors to BISHOP & CO.,

Manufacturers Wholesale and Retail Dealers in

Stoves, Ranges, Furnaces and Tinware.

Copper, Brass and Sheet Iron Work a Specialty.

No. 28 Pleasant Street,
WORCESTER, MASS.

L. B. HOLT,
·P·A·I·N·T·E·R·

DEALER IN

Paints, Oils, Varnishes and Glass.

GRAINING AND HARDWOOD FINISHING.

626 MAIN STREET.

GLASS SETTING A SPECIALTY

MASSAGE AND ELECTRIC TREATMENT for Ladies and Gentlemen at their residences. Appointment by telephone or at the office of JENSEN'S Turkish and Russian Baths, 1 Sudbury St., opp. Bay State House.

LOBSTER IN ASPIC.

Remove the meat from two two-pound lobsters, and make three cupfuls stock from the body, bones and tougher pieces. Allow the bones, etc., to remain in cold water for a few minutes then cook twenty minutes. Use the small body bones, not the shells. Add to this stock three cupfuls chicken stock ; add also one and a half tablespoonful lemon juice, a half teaspoonful celery salt, a few grains cayenne, a small piece lemon rind, using only the thin, yellow skin, a slight grating nutmeg, salt and pepper to taste. Soak one and a half box gelatine in a cup cold water, and add it to the stock, which must be cold, with the whites two eggs slightly beaten, and the shells broken in pieces. Place over the fire and stir till it boils, then set it back and simmer fifteen minutes. Remove the scum and strain through a flannel or double cheese cloth ; fill a mold partly full of this jelly and when firm lay in the lobster meat, add the remainder of the jelly gradually, and allow it to get firm.

OYSTERS, A LA THORNDIKE.

One pint oysters, one and a half tablespoonful butter half teaspoonful salt, a few grains cayenne, slight grating nutmeg, one and a half tablespoonfuls brandy (if liked), quarter cup cream and the yolks two eggs slighly beaten. Wash the oysters by pouring over them a quarter cup cold water, then drain thoroughly. Melt butter in a blazer, or granite saucepan, add oysters, salt, pepper, nutmeg, and cook about four minutes, then add brandy and the larger part of the cream, combining the remainder with the yolks, which must also be added to the oysters. Cook till the oysters are plump and their edges curl. Serve on zephyrettes which have been heated in the oven.

One 15 cent bottle of EKLUND'S JUNIPER BERRY EXTRACT will make four gallons of home brewed Juniper Beer, the best temperance drink to-day. Manufactured by C. A, EKLUND & CO., 5 Thomas St., and 101 Green St., Worcester, Mass.

CHARLES A. CUMMINGS,
Locksmith and Bellhanger,

REPAIRS SAFE LOCKS AND CHANGES COMBINATIONS.

All kinds of Bell Hanging and Repairing, Sharpens Shears and Cutlery, Repairs Carpet Sweepers, Clothes Wringers, etc.

NO. 16 MECHANIC ST.,   WORCESTER, MASS.

E. A. HARWOOD,
Cabinet Maker and Upholsterer.

ALL KINDS OF FURNITURE REPAIRED AND MIRROR PLATES PUT IN.

Also Saw Filing, Shears and Scissors Sharpened. Keys Fitted, Locks and Spirit Levels Repaired. Also my Industrial Class for Training Boys in the Use of Tools.

No. 22 1-2 PLEASANT St., U One Flight,

P. O. Box No. 308.   WORCESTER, MASS.

Book Binding.

We have every facility for re-binding and repairing old books of every description.

Our methods and materials are first class and our prices are reasonable.

J. S. WESBY & SONS,

Office, 387 MAIN ST.,   WORCESTER, MASS.

SULPHUR BATHS at JENSEN'S Turkish and Russian Bath Establishment
1 Sudbury St., opp. Bay State House. Telephone connection.

FISH A LA CREME.

Two pounds cod or haddock, cleaned and wiped with a wet cloth. Put it into a kettle of boiling water with one tablespoonful each of salt and vinegar. When the fish separates easily from the bones take it up and drain it, then pick it apart with a silver fork, spread on a platter and sprinkle with salt and pepper. Make one pint of white sauce like that on page 66, and pour it over the fish. Mix cup cracker crumbs and a third cup melted butter, and spreread it over the fish. Put into a hot oven and cook till the crumbs are nicely browned. Garnish with small sprays of parsley.

WELSH RAREBIT.

Put one tablespoonful butter into a chafing dish; when melted add a half pound cheese cut fine, one saltspoonful salt, a quarter saltspoonful cayenne. When creamy add gradually a half cup cream with the beaten yolks of two eggs. When slightly thick, like custard, pour over any kind of thin, delicate crackers, which have been heated. Mustard may be used if liked. This may be made in a saucepan set in hot water, on the stove.

LOBSTER SAUCE.

Cream half cup butter, add the yolks of two eggs and beat well; add the juice of half a lemon, one saltspoonful salt, a few grains cayenne and slowly add a third cup boiling water, cook over hot water, till it thickens slightly. Add a third cup lobster meat cut into dice.

EKLUND'S JUNIPER BERRY EXTRACT is made from juniper berries in their most purified state, and as juniper berries contain great medical and blood- purifying properties, we claim Juniper Beer to be the most healthful drink in the market.
C. A. EKLUND & CO., WORCESTER, MASS.

Whether you want
Little or Much Insurance,

— GO TO —

A. C. MUNROE,

Insurance Dealer,

ROOM 4, CLARK'S BLOCK,   492 MAIN STREET,

WORCESTER, MASS.

TELEPHONE NUMBERS.

Office, 378-5.   Residence, 272-3

Cabinet, Dry Hot Air, and Steam Baths for ladies and gentlemen at JENSEN'S SANITARY BATHING-ESTABLISHMENT, 1 Sudbury street, opp. Bay State House. Telephone connection.

OYSTERS AND TRIPE.

Wash, and put into boiling water one pound honeycomb tripe and cook twenty minutes; then drain and cut it into pieces about an inch square. Wash and drain a pint of oysters; make one pint white sauce (see rule for baked halibut, page 66). Put the oysters in a saucepan without any liquor, and cook till they are plump and the edges curl; add them with the tripe to the white sauce. Serve on toast. One-half this rule is sufficient for four or five people.

SCALLOPED OYSTERS.

One pint solid oysters washed and drained, one third cup melted butter, one cup cracker or stale bread crumbs, moistened in the melted butter. Butter a shallow dish, put in a layer of crumbs, then a layer of oysters, season with salt and pepper, and pour over three tablespoonfuls of the liquor, or milk, and if you like, add Worcestershire sauce, lemon juice, wine, or mace; then put in another layer of crumbs, then oysters, seasoning, and the three tablespoonfuls of milk, with a thick layer of crumbs on top. Bake in a hot oven about twenty minutes, or till the crumbs are brown.

HALIBUT FISH BALLS.

Combine equal quantities of cooked halibut, minced fine, and hot mashed potato; to a pint of the mixture add one teaspoonful butter and a beaten egg; season with salt and pepper. Fry like other fish balls, or dip in melted butter and bake.

Eklund's Swedish Pine Perfume, and Triple Extracts for the Handkerchief are of the finest quality, and are sold in bulk and one ounce bottles, at 5 Thomas street, and 101 Green street, Worcester, Mass.

WORCESTER STORAGE CO.
Incorporated 1889.

Warehouse at 29 Gold St. Court.

FOR THE STORAGE OF

Furniture, Pianos, Mirrors,

Statuary, Paintings, Trunks, Merchandise, Carriages, etc., etc., at lowest rates.   Packing and Shipping.

The Company owns its own vans, built expressly for the business, uses its own drivers and helpers for the removal of the contents of a dwelling house or other property, for storage in the Warehouse, or from one residence to another, and will execute all orders with promptness and despatch.

Persons desiring STORAGE OF ANY KIND are invited to visit the warehouse where full particulars may be obtained.

C. C. BROWN, Superintendent.

HORACE WYMAN, President.

H. WINFIELD WYMAN, Treasurer.

Telephone 642-3.

STAR LUNCH ROOM, 436 1-2 Main St. Open all Night. Hot Coffee in Insulated Tanks, Ice Cream, Cake and Sandwiches of all kinds furnished to Parties and Societies at short notice. F. E. & W. E. MARSHALL, Proprietors.

CLAM FRITTERS.

Drain the clams and chop the hard part; use the liquor to make fritter batter; add the clams, and fry by small spoonfuls in hot fat. Clams in the shell should be steamed till the shells open, then take them out and drain, cut off part of the neck and dip each one in the batter and fry.

BATTER.

Yolks of two eggs well beaten; add a half cup milk or water. or clam juice, one tablespoonful olive oil, one saltspoonful salt, one cup pastry flour, or enough to make it almost a drop batter. When ready to use add whites of the eggs beaten very stiff. If for fruit add one one teaspoonful sugar; if for clams, etc., add one tablespoonful lemon juice, or vinegar.

MEAT AND FISH SAUCES.

DRAWN BUTTER SAUCE.

One pint hot water, two tablespoonfuls butter, two of flour, half teaspoonful salt, half saltspoonful pepper. Put the butter in a saucepan; when melted add the dry flour and mix well; add the hot water a little at a time, and stir rapidly as it thickens, beating out all the lumps. Add salt and pepper, and lumps of butter if liked.

A variety of sauces may be made from this.

FOR BOILED MUTTON, add six tablespoonfuls capers.

FOR BAKED OR BOILED FISH, add two or three hard boiled eggs, sliced or chopped.

FOR BOILED FOWLS, add juice and pulp of large lemon.

One 25 cent bottle of EKLUND'S JUNIPER BERRY EXTRACT makes 6 gallons home brewed Juniper Beer, a blood purifier and a strengthening tonic. Sold by grocers and by C. A. EKLUND & CO., 5 Thomas St., and 101 Green St., Worcester, Mass.

DELIVERED IN ANY PART OF THE CITY:

HOME MADE CANDIES

AT WHOLESALE AND RETAIL.

Made on the premises, of Strictly Pure Materials. Always fresh and good, at

F. N. OXLEY'S DRUG STORE,

648 MAIN STREET,

WORCESTER, - MASS.

BAY STATE PLATING CO.,

Gold, Silver, Nickel and Aluminum

PLATING WORKS.

ELECTRO-PLATING IN ALL ITS BRANCHES.

Table Ware, Jewelry, Bird Cages, Fire Arms, Machinery, Models, Bicycles, Polished and Plated. Polishing, Bronzing, Lacquering of all kinds.
Particular Attention given to Jewelers' Work and Band Instruments. All work Hand Finished.

13 MECHANIC STREET, WORCESTER, MASS.

Star Lunch Room, 436½ Main street, F. E. & W. E. Marshall, Proprietors.— Open all night. Home-made Bread, Pies, Raised Doughnuts and Cream Rolls fresh every afternoon, cold sliced Ham, cold Roast Chicken and cold Roast Turkey can be obtained at any time. Dainty lunches a specialty.

BRAISED BEEF.

A slice from the top of the round, weighing about three pounds, an inch and a half thick. Wipe, season with salt and pepper, cut gashes in the slice an inch apart and half an inch deep, and fill the gashes with stuffing made as directed below. Roll up and skewer, or tie, putting in a few stitches, if necessary. Season again, dredge with flour and brown all over in salt pork fat, being careful not to pierce it with the fork. Place in a deep pan, on a bed of vegetables, using for this one-third cup carrots cut into dice, three slices onion and a bit of bay leaf. Pour on three cups boiling water; cover tightly and cook three hours, basting occasionally and turning the meat over a short time before it is done. When done take out meat and vegetables. Put into a saucepan a tablespoonful butter, add a tablespoonful dry flour, stir well and add gradually the liquor the meat was cooked in; season if necessary and strain. If too thick, add hot water. Put the meat on a platter, place the vegetables around it, and pour the gravy over the meat.

STUFFING.

To one-third cup cracker crumbs add one scant tablespoonful butter, one saltspoonful salt, one-fourth saltspoonful pepper, and one-half teaspoonful poultry seasoning. Moisten with four tablespoonfuls hot milk, or water.

BROWN SAUCE.

One pint hot stock, half teaspoonful salt, two tablespoonfuls minced onion, two of butter, two of flour, half saltspoonful pepper, 1 tablespoonful lemon juice. Mince the onion and fry it in the butter five minutes. Be careful not to burn it. When the butter is brown add dry flour and stir well; add the hot stock, a little at a time, stirring it rapidly, and beating out all the lumps; add salt, pepper and lemon juice. Simmer three or four minutes and strain.

Ask your druggist or grocer for **Eklunds "Genuine Swedish Pine Oil Soap."** This Soap is made from the very finest Oils and hygienic ingredients, by C. A. Eklund & Co., Worcester, Mass.

When you Paint
Your Houses,

USE THE

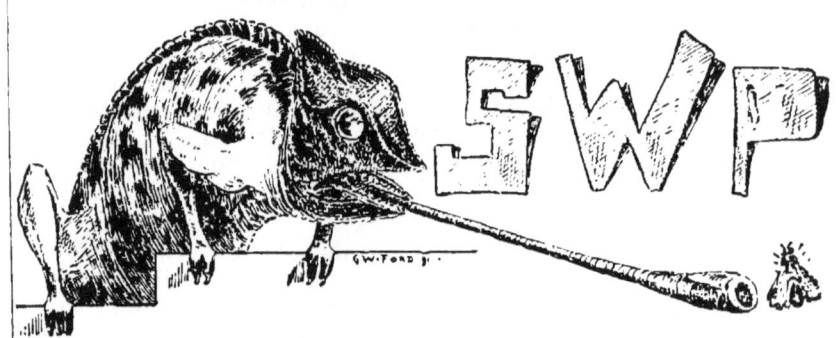

THE SHERWIN-WILLIAMS PAINT.
Covers Most, Looks Best, Wears Longest, Most Economical, Full Measure.

SOLD BY
THE ATHERTON PAINT CO.
9 Pleasant Street,   WORCESTER, MASS

Star Lunch Room, 436½ Main street, F. E. & W. E. Marshall, Prop'rs. Best cup of Coffee, with rich cream, in the city, for five cents. Dainty lunches served at any hour of the day or night. Home-made Bread and Pies a specialty. Open all night.

FRICASSEE OF LAMB.

Three pounds lamb or young mutton, from the fore quarter or the neck. Wipe with a wet cloth and cut into pieces suitable for serving; cover with hot water and cook slowly till tender. When done remove meat from the liquor; season the meat with salt and pepper, dredge with flour and brown in butter. Arrange on a platter and pour over it

BROWN SAUCE.

Brown two tablespoonfuls butter, add two rounding tablespoonfuls flour; pour on slowly, a little at a time, the liquor in which the lamb has been cooked, first removing the fat. Season with salt and pepper.

MUSHROOM SAUCE.

To the above sauce add a half can of mushrooms, whole or quartered, and simmer five minutes. The sauce may be made darker by adding a small quantity caramel, which may be purchased of druggists or grocers.

HAMBURG STEAKS.

Chop one pound lean beef, add to it one tablespoonful onion juice, half teaspoonful salt, and a quarter teaspoonful black pepper; mix well. Moisten the hands in cold water, take two tablespoonfuls of the mixture and form with the hands into small round cakes or steaks. This quantity should make eight. Put two tablespoonfuls butter into a frying pan when hot put in the steaks, brown on one side, then turn and brown on the other. Dish them, add a teaspoonful flour to the butter remaining in the pan, mix until smooth, add a half pint of boiling water slowly, stir constantly until it boils; add salt and pepper, and if you like, a tablespoonful of Worcestershire sauce; pour this over the steaks and serve, or they may be broiled same as plain steak, seasoned with salt and pepper and spread with butter.

Genuine Swedish Pine Leaf Oil has proved to be practically efficient as an inhalation agent for the lungs in Consumption Asthma and all pulmonary diseases of the chest, also for Rheumatism, Gout and Neuralgia, by adding 1 to 2 teaspoonfuls to a common hot water bath. C. A. Eklund & Co., sole importers for U. S. A.

T. A. PETERSON COMPANY,

Wholesale and Retail Dealers in

PLAIN AND ARTISTIC
Wall Papers, Window Shades
AND PICTURE MOULDINGS.

Paper Hanging and Decorating done in first-class manner, at reasonable prices and satisfaction guaranteed.

EXTRA AND ODD SIZE WINDOW SHADES MADE TO ORDER.

At our Green street store, in addition to Wall Paper, &c., we carry a full line of

Paints, Oils, Varnishes and Colors.

HEADQUARTERS
205 MAIN STREET, - 3 THOMAS STREET.
BRANCH STORE,
109 AND 111 GREEN STREET.

T. A. PETERSON COMPANY.

If you want the Best Coffee procurable, try our Ankola Java, 40c lb. There is none better. Very strong and fine flavor.
D. A. HOWE, 273 MAIN ST., WORCESTER.

MUTTON HASH—TOMATO SAUCE.

Chop cold cooked mutton. Put one tablespoonful butter in a frying pan; when very brown add one tablespoonful flour, mix, add a half pint hot water, stir until it boils, add meat and seasoning, cook slowly ten minutes. Have ready some buttered toast, dish the hash on it and pour around it tomato sauce.

TOMATO SAUCE.

Put one tablespoonful butter in a frying pan, when melted add one tablespoonful flour, mix, and add a half pint strained stewed tomatoes; stir until it boils, add a half teaspoonful grated onion, salt and pepper to taste.

HAM BALLS.

Chop cold, cooked pieces of ham, season with pepper, chopped parsley, or a little sweet marjoram. Add four tablespoonfuls stale bread crumbs to one gill milk, stir and cook until thick, add the yolks two eggs, take from the fire and add one cup of the chopped ham, mix, and stand away to cool. When cold form into balls, dip into beaten egg, then in bread crumbs and fry in smoking hot fat.

PORK TENDERLOINS, WITH SWEET POTATOES.

Wipe tenderloins, remove some of the fat, put into a dripping pan and brown quickly in a hot oven; then season with salt, pepper and sage. Bake from forty to forty-five minutes, being sure that it is thoroughly done, and basting frequently with the fat in the pan. Pare six sweet potatoes, parboil for ten minutes, drain and put them in the pan with the meat and cook till tender, basting often. Serve with the meat in the center of the platter and the potatoes arranged around the outside.

Eklund's "Amykos Aseptin Soap," and "Savon Excelsior" are toilet soaps of the finest quality at popular prices, and should be found in the nursery and ladies' toilet. Sold everywhere. Manufactured by C. A. EKLUND & CO., Worcester, Mass.

VALLEY
Woolen Mill,
CHERRY VALLEY, MASS.

Manufacturers and Retailers

LADIES' DRESS GOODS,
Cloakings and Flannels.

COME TO OUR RETAIL SALESROOMS.

Buy direct from the Loom.
Buy at Wholesale Prices.
Save all Profits for Yourselves.

All purchasers of $3.00, or over, given free return tickets over Electric Road to Worcester.

CHANNING SMITH.

CANNELON.

Chop one pound of uncooked beef, add to it the yolk of an egg, a tablespoonful chopped parsley, a tablespoonful melted butter, two tablespoonfuls stale bread crumbs, a teaspoonful salt and a quarter teaspoonful pepper; mix all well and form into a roll about six inches long and four inches in diameter; wrap in greased paper and bake in a quick oven thirty minutes. When done remove the paper and serve on a heated dish with brown sauce poured around it.

SMOTHERED MEAT.

The tough end of sirloin steaks and other pieces not fit for broiling may be chopped, seasoned with salt and pepper, and a few bits of butter; put this in a baking pan, cover with another, and bake in a quick oven about twenty minutes. Serve with its own gravy.

BEEF SAUSAGE.

Chop one pound uncooked lean beef and a quarter pound suet, mix and add a teaspoonful salt, a quarter teaspoonful white pepper, and a half teaspoonful sage, mix again, make into small round cakes and dredge with flour. Put two tablespoonfuls dripping in a frying pan, add a slice onion, cook until the onion turns a delicate brown, then fry the cakes quickly on both sides and serve very hot.

THE WORCESTER
Safe Deposit and Trust Company

✴ TRANSACTS A ✴

General Banking Business,

Receives deposits subject to check at sight, and allows
Interest on Daily Balances of $100
and upwards at the rate of two per cent. per annum.

Collections Made on all Avaliable Points.
Acts as Trustee under Wills and Trust Deeds.

NEW SAFE DEPOSIT VAULTS.

SAFES TO RENT at $5 to $50 per year.

BOARD OF DIRECTORS.

Warren Williams, Worcester.   E. D. Buffington, Worcester,
John H. Coes, Worcester,   Edward F. Bisco, Worcester,
Edwin T. Marble, Worcester,   Henry F. Harris, Worcester,
Charles S. Barton, Worcester.

EDWARD F. BISCO, Pres.   SAMUEL H. CLARY, Sec'y.

OFFICE HOURS.

9 a. m to 4 p. m.   Saturdays, 9 a. m. to 1 p. m.

Have you ever tried the New England Baking Powder? If not, try one pound, price 25c lb. Equal to either Royal or Cleveland's. Sold only by D. A. HOWE, 273 MAIN STREET.

MAYONNAISE DRESSING.

One teaspoonful mustard, one of sugar, one-half teaspoonful salt, one-fourth saltspoonful cayenne, one pint olive oil, yolks two raw eggs, three tablespoonfuls vinegar, three of lemon juice. Mix the first four ingredients in a quart bowl, add the yolks, mix well, then add a half teaspoonful oil and beat with a Dover egg beater till well mixed, continue adding a half teaspoonful of oil at a time beating after each addition until thick, then thin it with part of the lemon juice, then add the oil, a tablespoonful at a time, till thick, then the remainder of the lemon juice, then add oil and vinegar alternately till all are used. The dressing should be quite thick when done. Beat the whites of the two eggs till very stiff, adding enough to the dressing to make it the right consistency, or stiff enough when taken up on a spoon to drop and not run. Do all beating with a Dover or Keystone beater. Should the mixture curdle put two fresh yolks into a bowl, using the curdled mixture, a little at a time, just as you would oil, thinning out when necessary, with lemon juice and vinegar. Add no more seasoning unless necessary. Always have oil, eggs and bowl very cold.

FRENCH DRESSING.

One-eighth teaspoonful salt, one saltspoonful pepper, a quarter teaspoonful onion juice, one teaspoonful made mustard, one tablespoonful vinegar, three of olive oil. Mix in the order given, adding the vinegar slowly, and lastly, the oil, slowly. This dressing is suitable for vegetable or egg salads.

C. A. EKLUND & CO., makers of Eklund's Juniper Berry Extract, Perfumes and Toilet Soaps give liberal discount to wholesale and retail dealers. Try to handle their goods and see how readily they sell. Office 5 Thomas St., Worcester, Mass.

KODAKS.

Cameras of Every Description

BOUGHT AND SOLD.

OLD CAMERAS TAKEN IN TRADE.

Latest Styles, Lowest Prices, and a complete line of Photograph Materials.
Instructions and use of dark-room free.

THE WORCESTER SUPPLY CO.
7 PLEASANT ST.,   WORCESTER, MASS.

Union Clean Towel Supply Co.,
9 AND 11 PRESCOTT ST.,
WORCESTER - MASS.

ALL WORK DONE BY HAND.

Why have the confusion of Wash Day, when we will wash 36 pieces for 35 cents? or for washing and ironing plain, 35 cents per dozen.

Goods entirely at the owner's risk, in case of Fire.

Every Washing done by itself.
We wash Blankets in the old English way, and they are made as Soft and Clean as new.

Try our Flavored Mocha Coffee at 25c lb. It is the best Coffee sold for the money. People who can not drink other Coffee, can drink this without injury.
D. A. HOWE, 273 Main St., Worcester.

VEAL LOAF.

Chop three and a half pounds of uncooked veal and a half pound of ham, add one cup of stale bread crumbs, one teaspoonful of salt, one of onion juice, a half teaspoonful of cloves, same of sage and pepper, and two well beaten eggs; mix all well together and form into a square loaf. Put it in a baking pan, brush it over with egg, and bake in a slow oven for two hours, basting two or three times with melted butter. Serve cold, cut in thin slices.

CURRY OF MUTTON.

Chop one pint of cold cooked mutton; put one tablespoonful ot butter in a frying pan; when melted, add a tablespoonful of flour and stir until smooth; add half a pint of boiling water, stir until it boils; add the meat, a teaspoonful of curry powder and a half teaspoonful of salt; stir until thoroughly heated, then heap it in the center of a meat dish, and put around it a border of nicely boiled rice.

MUTTON SAUSAGES.

Chop one pint of cold cooked mutton, three ounces of beef suet, and six raw oysters; mix, add a half cup of bread crumbs, one egg slightly beaten, salt, pepper, and a quarter teaspoonful of mace, and if convenient, a teaspoonful of anchovy paste; mix all thoroughly together into small round cakes, and fry in butter. These are very nice with tomato sauce.

Eklund's "Medicated Aromatic Soap" is a dentifrice of merit as well as a very fine toilet soap. It has an agreeable odor and is a necessity for every toilet. Sold by Druggists and Grocers. C. A. EKLUND & CO., Worcester, Mass., Sole Manufacturers.

HORACE B. VERRY,
Attorney and Counsellor at Law,

Room 15, Walker Building.

405 MAIN STREET,   **WORCESTER, MASS.**

J. D. SISSON,
Sanitary Plumbing, Ventilation,
✢ STEAM AND GAS PIPING. ✢

7 CENTRAL ST.,   **WORCESTER, MASS.**

C. E. GALLAGHER & CO.

Are now prepared to submit for inspection, the choicest assortment of Exclusive and Artistic

MILLINERY

to be found in the city. Our Sales Ladies are always pleased to show, even if you don't care to purchase. All Ladies desiring to see the Latest and Prettiest Creations of the Milliner's Art are cordially invited to visit our store at

~ 31 PLEASANT STREET. ~

A FEW DOORS FROM MAIN STREET.

MISS C. E. GALLAGHER & CO.

Try a pound of our 50c Formosa Tea, it has a rich delicate flavor,
and will please you.

D. A. HOWE.   273 MAIN ST., WORCESTER.

SALMON SALAD.

Prepare in the same way with cooked or canned salmon, free from bones, skin and oil.

OYSTER SALAD.

Clean one pint white celery and cut into fine pieces. Season with salt. Parboil one pint oysters, drain, and when cold mix them with a French dressing. Put a layer of shredded lettuce in a salad bowl, sprinkle with a French dressing; add the oysters and celery, cover with a mayonnaise dressing, and garnish with pickled barberries.

SPINACH SALAD.

Wash very thoroughly a half peck spinach in a small amount boiling salted water, till tender. A saltspoonful soda or a few drops ammonia will prevent it losing its green color. When done drain thoroughly, pressing it with a knife to get out all the water; chop it fine add two tablespoonfuls melted butter, with salt, pepper and lemon juice to taste. Pack into small cup-shaped molds, buttering them slightly first, and chill. Serve on thin slices cold tongue: put a spoonful salad dressing on the top of each.

TOMATO SALAD.

To one can stewed or strained tomatoes add one teaspoonful salt, three quarters box gelatine, which has been soaked till soft, in a half cup cold water, and dissolved in a half cup boiling water. Mould in round cups, about two-thirds full; serve on lettuce leaves, and put on the top of each some mayonnaise or cream dressing. Before filling rinse the moulds with cold water; do not wipe them.

Blank Books of all kinds, also Blank Books made to order.

WILLIAM W. LEWIS,   505 Main Street

Ye WEBSTER STUDIO.

CABINET PHOTOS, BEST QUALITY, $2 PER DOZEN

SPECIAL FOR MARCH

WEBSTER, FINE PHOTOGRAPHY
393——MAIN STREET.——393

A. B. BRUNELL,

Electro, Gold, Silver and Nickel Plater.

ELECTRO PLATING AND POLISHING of Every Description

10 BARTON PLACE.

WORCESTER, - MASS.

We have all grades of Tea as follows : Formosa, Japans, (Basket and Pan dried), English Breakfasts, Amoys, Fouchons, Young Hyson, Gunpowder, Ceylons, Assam and Orange Pearl. Fresh importations and the best of goods.
D. A. HOWE, 273 Main St., Worcester, Mass.

CREAM SALAD DRESSING.

One and one-half cups fresh, thick cream, yolks two hard boiled eggs, one teaspoonful sugar, three-fourths teaspoonful salt, one-half saltspoonful cayenne, three-fourths teaspoonful mustard, one and one-half tablespoonful vinegar. Rub the yolks to a smooth paste, gradually add the salt, sugar, mustard and vinegar. The cream should be very cold ; beat it with an egg beater until smooth and rather thick. Stir this, a spoonful at a time, into the egg mixture, and use it the same as a mayonnaise.

BOILED SALAD DRESSING.

Melt one tablespoonful butter in a saucepan, add one tabespoonful flour ; cook together till frothy, but not brown ; add gradually a half cup vinegar and continue cooking till the mixture thickens, then remove from the stove. Mix thoroughly one teaspoonful each, salt, sugar and mustard, and a few grains cayenne, and stir into the vinegar sauce, stirring until smooth. Heat one cup milk in a double boiler, add two beaten egg yolks, mix well and cook like a soft custard, stirring constantly. When slightly thickened remove the upper boiler and gradually mix the custard with the vinegar sauce. Beat it with an egg beater till smooth and strain before it cools. Put it away in glass jars closely covered, and it will keep for weeks in a cool place.

CHICKEN SALAD.

One pint each of cold boiled or roasted chicken and celery, or half as much celery as chicken. Cut the chicken into quarter inch dice. Scrape, wash, and cut the celery in dice. Mix and marinate with a French dressing, and keep on ice until ready to serve. Make a mayonnaise dressing, and mix part of it with the chicken ; arrange the salad in a dish, pour the remainder of the dressing over it, and garnish with celery leaves or lettuce.

Baker's Lemon and Orange are extracted from the rind of the fruit, and leave that grateful and agreeable taste without the odor of turpentine frequently found in many kinds made from poisonous oils and acids toned with Cayenne pepper.

O. DALBECK,

MANUFACTURER OF

Store, Saloon and Druggists' Fixtures.

CABINET WORK
of Every Description.

Window and Door Screens,

Furniture Repairing.

**91 EXCHANGE ST.,
WORCESTER, - MASS.**

LEWIS H. SCOTT,

Manufacturer of
SILK, LINEN and COTTON

ELASTIC STOCKINGS,

For the Support of Varicose Veins, Swelled Limbs, Weak Joints, Rheumatism, etc.

Thigh Hose,
Knee Caps,
Leggins,
Abdominal Belts,

made of the Best Imported Rubber Thread.

Send for Price List.

**515 Main St.,
Worcester, Mass.**

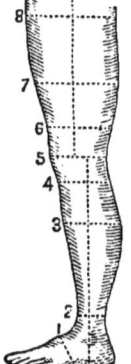

School of English Speech,
34 FRONT ST., WORCESTER.

Seventh Year. Class and Private Instruction in Reading, Shakespeare, English, Pronunciation, Deep Breathing, Standing, Walking and Lifting of the Vital Organs. Special exercise for increasing the Chest Measurement and decreasing the Abdominal Measurement. Persons who may wish to know about the practical results of the work in Lung Gymnastics and also about the exercises for Grace, Health and Strength, will be referred to members of the classes in this work.

Address MRS. CUTLER, SCHOOL OF ENGLISH SPEECH.

MISS MORIARTY.
LADIES' HAIR DRESSING,
Facial Massage and Manicure.

Removing Superfluous Hair, Warts and Moulds with Electricity.

ROOM 14, BURNSIDE BLOCK,

339 MAIN STREET.

APPLE SNOW.

Peel and grate one large sour apple, sprinkling over it a small cupful powdered sugar as you grate it, to keep it from turning dark. Break into this whites of two eggs and beat it all constantly for half an hour. Take care to have it in a large bowl as it beats up very stiff and light. Heap this in a glass dish and pour a fine smooth custard around it and serve. A very delicate dessert.

CHARLOTTE RUSSE.

Soak one-fourth box gelatine in one-fourth cup cold water. Line a pint mold with lady fingers. Chill and whip one pint cream; set bowl in ice water; sift over the whipped cream one-third cup powdered sugar, add one teaspoonful vanilla and one tablespoonful white wine. Dissolve gelatine in one-quarter cup boiling water. Strain it into the cream and beat rapidly. When nearly stiff pour into molds and set away to cool.

CHARLOTTE RUSSE No. 2.

One pound lady fingers, one quart sweet cream, three-fourths cup powdered sugar, two teaspoonfuls vanilla. Split and trim the cakes, and fit neatly in the bottom and sides of two quart molds. Whip the cream to a stiff froth, after it has been sweeetned and flavored; fill the molds, lay the cakes closely together on the top and set on ice till needed. The edges of the cake may be moistened with a little jelly, that the shape may be more easily retained.

The "Bread which strengthens men's hearts" is made from

Butterfly Flour,

and to obtain best results from the recipes on the oppposite page use ONLY

BUTTERFLY.

ARTHUR E. GRAY,   N. E. Agent.

Diploma of Honorable Mention awarded by Board of Lady Managers of World's Columbian Exhibition.

WHITE & OSTERBERG
MANUFACTURING UPHOLSTERERS,

4 AUSTIN STREET,
Cor. MAIN ST.

Couches, Turkish Chairs, Divans, Sofas, etc., to order.

Hair Mattresses, Cushions, for Bay Windows, Cars, Chairs, etc.

REPAIRING in all its branches.

FANCY GOODS AND NOVELTIES.
WILLIAM W. LEWIS,   505 Main Street.

LOBSTER SALAD.

Cut one pint lobster meat into dice, season with a French dressing and keep on ice until ready to serve, then mix with half of the mayonnaise dressing. Make nests or cups of the crisp lettuce leaves; break the poorer lettuce leaves and mix with the lobster. Put a large spoonful of the lobster in each leaf, with a tablespoonful of the mayonnaise on top.

SALAD SANDWICHES.

Mix a small quantity of mayonnaise dressing with finely cut lobster or chicken. Cover a small slice of bread with lettuce, then the salad, lettuce, and bread again. Wrap them in tin foil, or oiled paper, and serve at picnics, or when traveling.

LOBSTER SALAD.

Cut the lobster fine and moisten it slightly with a mayonnaise dressing. Pack it closely in a buttered mould, and keep on ice till ready to serve. Then turn out on a platter and spread the top and sides with a thick mayonnaise. Cut lettuce into half inch strips and pile lightly around the base. Put slices of red radish or rings of beet here and there among the green.

CABBAGE SALAD.

Cut half the white cabbage in very thin strips, sprinkle with salt, put it between two plates, and let it stand one hour. Drain off the water, sprinkle it with a French dressing; pile it lightly in a dome-shaped mass. Cut cold beets in thin slices, separate into rings and arrange them in an overlapping border around the base.

Wedding and Card Engraving, also all kinds of Printing.
WILLIAM W. LEWIS,   505 Main Street.

C. G. BORMAN,

DEALER IN

Wall Papers, - Window Shades,

ROOM MOULDINGS, ETC.

A large stock always on hand, of the latest styles and at the lowest prices such goods can be bought. All work guaranteed to be first-class.

30 Bellevue St., cor Chandler,   WORCESTER, MASS.

Antique Furniture
Put in Repair.
5 O'Clock Tea Tables.
Furniture Made.

CABINET WORK
. . . IN ITS . . .
SPECIAL BRANCHES.

J. W. LORING & SON,

86 Foster Street,

J. W. LORING.
E. H. LORING.

WORCESTER, MASS.

FOR LUNCH, TRY H. W. & CO. STAR LUNCH.
FINEST BISCUIT ON THE MARKET.

STRAWBERRY OR RASPBERRY SPONGE.

One quart strawberries or raspberries, a half box gelatine, one and a half cups water, one cup sugar, juice one lemon, beaten whites of four eggs. Soak gelatine in one-half cup of the water. Mash the berries and add half the sugar to them. Boil remainder of sugar and cup of water gently twenty minutes. Rub berries through a hair sieve. Add gelatine to boiling syrup, take from the fire and add berry juice. Place the bowl in pan of ice water and beat with egg beater five minutes. Add beaten whites and beat till it begins to thicken. Pour into well wet molds and set on ice. Serve with cream. Easily made and good.

CREAM SAUCE (with wine.)

One-fourth cup butter creamed with a half cup powdered sugar. Just before serving add two tablespoonfuls white wine one teaspoonful vanilla, and two tablespoonfuls cream.

SUBSTITUTE FOR CREAM.

Boil three fourths of a pint sweet milk; beat yolk of one egg, and a level teaspoonful flour with sugar enough to make the cream very sweet. When the milk boils stir this into it and let cool; flavor to taste. For puddings in which eggs are used this is almost as good as rich cream, and preferable to thin cream.

EXCELLENT PUDDING SAUCE.

Two coffee cups sugar, three-fourths coffee cup butter; rub to a cream. When well mixed stir in a half teacup boiled cider, a little at a time. Just before serving set in a kettle boiling water until hot, but not boiling.

BAKER'S EXTRACTS

Are double the strength of ordinary extracts, which makes them the most economical to use.

A SECRET ABOUT MINCE PIE.

A man was buying mince meat at the **Protective Union,** when the clerk remarked with animation, "**O, what is as good as Mince Pie? I could eat a piece just now.**" Just then a cloud passed over his face, as he continued, "But it disagrees with my stomach."

The customer at once informed him that he might **fearlessly** eat mince pie, if he would only use Bardwell's "Q. R." for Dyspepsia. It stops that burning sensation at the pit of the stomach, and removes that **imaginary** lump in the throat, and that nauseas, sour taste; and for **belching**—well, just try it once. Sold by Druggists and Grocers. Trial size, 15 cents. Regular size, 25 cents.

Mr. S. A. Pratt, of the **Protective Union,** No. 24 Front Street, after selling the "Q. R." for **eight years,** recommends it very highly as an article of **real merit.**

GEO. A. STEVENS,

Dealer in all kinds of

Family Flour,

ALSO, ALL KINDS OF

❋ MEALS, ❋

Bread Meal, Rye Meal, Graham Meal, Oat Meal, Rolled Oats, etc.

36 AND 38 SOUTHBRIDGE ST.,
WORCESTER, MASS.

USE H. W. J. & CO. BROWN BAKED BUTTER CRACKERS.

BAKED CUSTARD.

One quart milk, four beaten eggs, four tablespoonfuls sugar; flavor with lemon, vanilla or nutmeg; salt. Bake slowly, and do not let it remain too long in the oven.

CUSTARD SOUFFLE.

Rub two scant tablespoonfuls butter to a cream, add two scant tablespoonfuls flour. Pour over this gradually one cup hot milk, and cook eight minutes in a double boiler, stirring often. Beat yolks four eggs, add two tablespoonfuls sugar, stir into the milk and set away to cool. Half an hour before serving beat whites four eggs stiff, and add to mixture lightly. Bake in buttered pudding dish in a moderate oven thirty-six minutes. Serve at once.

BAVARIAN CREAM.

Whites of six eggs, beaten very light, one quart whipped cream, one ounce gelatine (soak one hour in cold water, drain and dissolve in a little hot water), flavor with one teaspoonful vanilla. Beat eggs and cream together, add sugar to sweeten, flavor, then add gelatine. Beat until it begins to thicken and pour into molds. Serve very cold with cream.

BOHEMIAN CREAM.

One quart cream, two tablespoonfuls sugar, one ounce gelatine dissolved. Whip half the cream to a stiff froth. Boil the other half with the sugar and a vanilla bean until flavor is extracted, or add vanilla extract after it is removed from the fire. Add the gelatine, and when cooled a little, the well beaten yolks of four eggs. Beat until it begins to stiffen, then beat in quickly the whipped cream. Pour in well wet molds and set on ice.

Full stock of Crepe Paper for Lamp Shades and Fancy Work.

WILLIAM W. LEWIS,   505 Main Street.

GO TO **GEO. JENNISON,**
DEALER IN
Fish, Oysters, Lobsters and Clams,
WHOLESALE AND RETAIL.

OYSTERS AND CLAMS Opened Fresh Every Day.

84 GREEN ST.

Telephone, 337-3

MISS M. A. DOHERTY,
MILLINERY PARLORS
Mourning Millinery a Specialty.

1 Chatham St., Cor. Main St.,   WORCESTER, MASS.

CHAS. A. MIDDLEMAS,
Practical Plumber
AND DEALER IN
PLUMBING MATERIALS
OF ALL KINDS.

SANITARY ✸ PLUMBING.

Allen Court, Cor. Main St.,

WORCESTER, - MASS.

ORIGINAL BERWICK SPONGE CAKE AT
H. W. JENNISON & CO., 64   66 MILLBURY ST.

FRUIT SAUCE.

Take one quart any kind ripe fruit, as red raspberries, strawberries or peaches; if the latter they must be very ripe. Pare and mash the fruit with a potato masher. Add one tablespoonful melted butter and one cup powdered sugar. Stir well and set on fire till warm.

HARD SAUCE.

Half cup butter well beaten; stir in slowly one cup fine sugar and beat to a cream. Pile on a plate and grate over a little nutmeg. Keep cool.

LEMON SAUCE.

Three-fourths cup sugar, half cups butter, one egg, the juice, and half the grated rind one lemon, one teaspoonful nutmeg and a half cup boiling water. Cream the butter and sugar and beat in the egg, whipped light, the lemon and the nutmeg. Beat hard, then add the water, put into a tin pail and set within the uncovered top of tea kettle, which must boil until the sauce is very hot, but not boiling. Stir constantly.

LEMON SAUCE No. 2.

Half cup butter, one cup sugar, one egg, the grated rind and juice of a lemon, one tablespoonful corn starch, one cup boiling water. Boil together a few moments and serve. This is very nice, and may be made by adding a half cup milk or cream. But when either milk or cream is used the butter should be omitted, and the milk should first be thickened with the corn starch.

SPEIRS MFG. CO., 279 Main St., Worcester, Mass. Manufacturers of Bicycles and dealers in all kinds of porting Goods.

Lincoln Holland, anager.

C. H. DERBY & CO.,
Practical Upholsterers.

HAIR MATTRESSES AND CUSHIONS
To Order and Made Over.

Furniture Re-Upholstered. ✳ **Carpet Work of All Kinds.**

Dwelling House Awnings of all kinds.
Wedding Canopies to Let.

531 MAIN STREET, - WORCESTER, MASS.

J. F. BIGELOW, 19 FOSTER ST., WORCESTER, MASS.
MANUFACTURER OF

It Kills but does not CRUSH the fly or other insect.
The insect can be killed on the most delicate wall paper or ceiling without soiling.
It is the only thing that kills the fly in a clean manner.

Once used, it will be found invaluable for Residences, Hotels, Offices, etc., etc.
It is made of fine, Spring-Steel, Plated Ware.
No household is complete without a FLY KILLER.

Jan. 8, 1895.

However well screened a house may be,
Tormenting flies you're sure to see.
Just make up your mind you'll be rid of the pest,
And the WIRE FLY KILLER will then do the rest.

Crockery, Kitchen Department Stores, Grocery and Hardware Dealers keep them.

ASK FOR THE KILLER.

ASK YOUR GROCER FOR A LOAF OF H. W. J. & CO. BREAD.

RUSSIAN CREAM.

Four eggs, one cup sugar, one quart milk, one half box gelatine dissolved in one pint warm water. Beat the yolks of eggs, add sugar, cook with the milk like custard. Take it off the stove, add beaten whites, stir well a few moments. Add gelatine and a teaspoonful strained lemon juice. Pour into well wet mold, and set on ice to harden. Serve with whipped or plain cream.

SPANISH CREAM.

One-half box gelatine, one quart milk, yolks three eggs, one small cup sugar; soak the gelatine in the milk for an hour, then put on the fire and stir as it warms; beat the yolks very light with the sugar, add to the scalding milk and heat to boiling point, stirring all the time. Strain into a mold and flavor with vanilla.

SAUCE.—Beat the whites of eggs to a stiff froth, three tablespoonfuls sugar; flavor with vanilla.

STRAWBERRY CREAM.

Mash one quart strawberries with one cup powdered sugar, and rub through a hair sieve. Dissolve one and a half ounces gelatine in one pint sweet milk. Strain, and add one pint whipped cream, and the berry juice. Pour in a wet mold and set on ice to form.

ANOTHER WAY.—One quart strawberries rubbed through a hair sieve, mix with three pints rich cream, and sweeten. Whip to a froth, add a half ounce dissolved gelatine. Serve in glasses.

Good Quality is Good Economy. It is poor economy to buy poor goods.
To have your food healthful as well as appetizing, use BAKER'S EXTRACTS.

Feathers, Down and Pillows a Specialty. We have the largest Steam Renovating facilities in the New England States. All our Feathers are gathered and shipped direct from the West. Our prices are in touch with the times.

We are dealers in Comforters, Feathers, Husk, Moss, Tow, Hair and Bedding of all kinds.

CHURCH SUPPERS, SOCIALS AND PICNIC PARTIES
Supplied on Short Notice, at

H. W. JENNISON & CO.

DELICIOUS PEACH PUDDING.

Fill a pudding dish with whole peeled peaches, and pour over them two cups water. Cover closely and bake until peaches are tender, then drain off the juice from the peaches and let stand until cool. Add to the juice one pint sweet milk, four well beaten eggs, a small cup flour with one teaspoonful baking powder mixed in it, one cup sugar, one tablespoonful melted butter and a little salt. Beat well three or four minutes, and pour over peaches in dish. Bake until a rich brown, and serve with cream.

PRUNE PUDDING.

One pound stewed prunes, whites four eggs, one cup sugar. After the prunes are stewed, drain off the juice, remove the stones and chop. Beat the eggs very stiff, add the sugar gradually, beating all the time; then stir in the chopped prunes. Bake twenty minutes. Serve cold with whipped cream flavored with wine.

SNOW PUDDING.

Dissolve a half box gelatine in one pint cold water; when soft add one pint boiling water, the grated rind and juice of two lemons, and two and a half cups sugar. Let stand until cold and begins to stiffen; then beat in the whites five eggs, well beaten. Pour into a mold and set on ice. Serve with custard sauce.

SAUCE.—One quart rich milk, yolks five eggs, with two extra eggs added; a half cup sugar. Flavor with vanilla.

GOLF. NEW, but POPULAR. Call at the SPEIRS MFG. CO., 279 Main Street, and see samples, etc.
LINCOLN HOLLAND, Manager.

LAWRENCE,
492 Main Street, - Worcester, Mass.

"You put in waisins?" "No." "Mrs. 'Umphrey's 'ceipt says so!" "Oh, say! let's go to LAWRENCE'S and have our pictures taken, making pies." "He can't take 'em." "Yes he can; he took a lovely one of Maudie, dancing, and my mamma went to Boston for her pictures, and three places here nobody knew 'em. Aunt Lou told her ' go to LAWRENCE,' and he made her splendid ones, look just like her. Papa says, ' best she ever had.' "

"Won't our mammas be s'prised to see our pictures, baking?" "LAWRENCE don't bake his pictures" "Why?" " 'Cause they are Well Done."

MISS A. V. CARBERRY,
CHIROPODIST.
Corns, Bunions and Ingrown Nails treated Without Pain.

MANICURE.

Burnside Building, Room 18.   339 MAIN STREET,
WORCESTER, MASS.

BREAD AND ROLLS delivered to all parts of the city, Fresh, Morning and Afternoon.

H. W. JENNISON & CO.

PLAIN SAUCE.

Half cup butter, one and a half cup sugar, rubbed to a cream. Add two well beaten eggs, and just before serving add enough boiling water to make a thick cream. Flavor with vanilla.

STRAWBERRY SAUCE.

One large tablespoonful butter beaten to a cream. Add gradually one and a half cups powdered sugar, and the beaten white of one egg. Beat till very light and just before serving add one pint mashed strawberries.

SLICED APPLE PIE.

Line a pie plate with pastry and fill with sliced tart apples. Sprinkle two tablespoonfuls sugar and grate a little nutmeg over the apples. Cover with a sheet of pastry with openings cut for the steam to escape.

DUTCH APPLE PUDDING.

One pint flour, one and a half teaspoonfuls baking powder, half teaspoonful salt. Rub a quarter cup butter into the flour, beat one egg light, add to it three-quarters cup cold water, and stir into the flour. Spread in well buttered shallow pans. Pare, core and quarter four or five sour apples, place them on the dough, and sprinkle over them two tablespoonfuls sugar. Bake twenty or thirty minutes. Serve at once with lemon sauce.

STEAMED BERRY PUDDING.

One cup sugar, two eggs, one and a half teaspoonful baking powder, two cups flour, one cup sweet milk, two cups berries. Steam about two hours.

This is our Ladies' Bicycle, a truly superb machine, by name "Majestic," with all it implies, and price, only $75, but it is strictly high grade. SPEIRS MFG. CO., 279 MAIN ST., WORCESTER. LINCOLN HOLLAND, Manager.

The Old Way

How shall our food be properly cooked? This is a question that is being considered now, more than at any time during the past.

Cooking Schools are being established almost everywhere, that those who have the important work of coooking to do can be taught how to do it.

One of the greatest contributors toward the success of this work is the introduction of Gas for fuel. Only a few years have elapsed since its general adoption for this purpose, and yet thousands of people can speak of its superior advantages over other fuel, especially in the Summer.

It does its work *quicker*, *better* and costing less than any other summer fuel. By the careful use of Gas, there is no doubt that a great saving in the cost of fuel is affected. The consumer should exercise a little supervision until habits of carefulness have been established. The gas should not be turned on until required and turned off directly, when done with. We will always be glad to give any information on the subject of cooking by Gas to all who may be interested.

The New Way

Worcester Gas Light Co.,
33 PEARL STREET.

For anything made in the Baker's line, call or address
H. W. JENNISON & CO., 64 & 66 Millbury St.
TELEPHONE 478-4.

BAKED BANANAS.

Use only fine, sound bananas. Loosen the bananas from the skin, so they can be removed easily after baking; replace and bake about half an hour, then remove from the skins and pour over them a sauce made by boiling a half cup sugar and a half cup water together for five minutes, then add a teaspoonful butter, and the juice of half a lemon.

ORANGE PUFFS.

Cream a third cup butter, add gradually one cup sugar, two eggs well beaten, and a half cup milk; add one and three-quarter cups pastry flour, with two scant teaspoonfuls baking powder; mix and beat thoroughly and bake in small tins fifteen or twenty minutes. Serve with orange sauce.

ORANGE SAUCE.

Beat the whites of three eggs till stiff, but not dry; add a cupful powdered sugar, the grated rind one orange, and the juice of two. This should be served at once, poured over the puffs. If liked, add also the juice of a lemon.

CHOCOLATE CAKE.

One half cup (scant) butter, creamed, one cup sugar, two eggs, whites and yolks beaten separately, half cup sweet milk, two cups flour, two teaspoonfuls baking powder. Boil together not quite a quarter cake chocolate grated, a half cup milk, yolk one egg, one cup sugar and one teaspoonful vanilla. When cool add to the above mixture. Bake in jelly tins and put boiled icing between the layers.

GOOD COOKING is one of the chief blessings of every home. To insure uniform results, BAKER'S EXTRACTS should always be used.

WHY NOT BE ON TIME?

The place to get your

CLOCKS REPAIRED

IS AT 543 MAIN STREET.

All work warranted. Will call at your house, office, or place of business, on receipt of postal.

N. L. RANDALL.

WILLCOX & GIBBS
IS THE ONLY
AUTOMATIC,
No Tenison, Silent, Sewing Machine.

MISS C. L. PERCY,
Sole Agent for Worcester and vicinity.
70 Pleasant St.

A Cozy, Pleasant place, where you can take plenty of time to select your Millinery, is at

MRS. L. A. PRATT'S
MILLINERY PARLORS,
49 PLEASANT STREET.

OLD MATERIALS worked over, and all done in the Latest Style.

Up One Flight.   Elevator.

GEO. D. WOODWARD, Prop.   GEO. C. PALMER, Sup't.

Globe Plating Company,
71 WINTER ST.,   WORCESTER, MASS.

ELECTRO PLATERS in Gold, Silver, Nickel and other Metals.

BRASSING AND LACQUERING.   POLISHING A SPECIALTY.

Chandeliers and Fire Irons Re-Gilded.

Cleveland's Superior Baking Powder.
Used and recommended by Mrs. C. E. Humphrey, Teacher of Cooking.

BOSTON PUDDING.

One cup sugar, two-thirds cup butter, or one quarter pound suet minced, one cup sweet milk, three cups flour, two teaspoonfuls baking powder, two tablespoonfuls molasses, one cup seeded raisins, a little salt. Boil four hours. One pint milk can be used instead of one cup, with bread crumbs soaked in it, and only one cup flour. Serve with rich liquid sauce.

BROWN BETTY.

Grease a pudding dish and place in the bottom a layer bread crumbs. Then nearly fill the dish with alternate layers crumbs and chopped or sliced apples, strewing brown sugar, cinnamon, and a little butter over each layer, topping off with crumbs. Bake one hour and serve with hard sauce.

CHERRY OR BLACKBERRY BREAD.

Stew cherries or blackberries, and sweeten to taste. Butter some slices stale bread with crusts cut off. Then put a layer of the buttered bread in the bottom of serving dish and pour over it hot stewed fruit. Repeat until dish is full, or fruit used. To be eaten cold, with cream.

PEACH COTTAGE PUDDING.

Stir sliced peaches into a batter made of a half cup sugar, three tablespoonfuls melted butter, one beaten egg, one cup milk, one pint flour, and one and a half teaspoonfuls baking powder. Bake in a loaf and serve with hard sauce.

WINE SAUCE.

Three quarters cup butter beaten to a cream, then add two cups powdered sugar. Beat well and stir in one tablespoonful corn starch wet in a half cup cold water. Cook until thick, then add a half cup wine.

TENNIS GOODS. We carry a full line RACKETS, NETS, SHOES, etc. **SPEIRS MFG. CO., 279 Main St.**

The Veteran Seer and Healer,

With Fifty Years' Experience and his other Gifts, makes him More than an Expert in all Female Diseases.

He has Lost only One Patient in 27 Years. Every Patient begins to be Well when they begin Treatment. No Guessing Here.

IS LOCATED AT

62 LINCOLN ST., WORCESTER, MASS.,

Where he continues to cure the sick and make the lame walk, the blind see and the deaf hear.

This great healer cures every disease that the human flesh is heir to and makes a specialty of all such diseases as other doctors cannot cure. This great healer has a power whereby he can diagnose your disease in five minutes, and will not touch you. Remember the number,

62 LINCOLN STREET, WORCESTER,

Where the sick and afflicted can consult with him free and be cured if they choose. This Great Healer has cured the following diseases, which are only a synopsis of the many that he has treated within the last fifty years: Consumption, in all its different stages, 2009 cases; Acute Rheumatism, 1863; Chronic Rheumatism, 1704; Neuralgia, 2713; Paralysis, in all its forms, over 3000 cases; Dyspepsia, 2901; Diseases of the Spine and Kidneys, 1927; Catarrh, 4023; Heart Disease, 142; Cancers, 192; Tumors, 379; Liver troubles, 1309, etc. I could continue this enumeration through those of different ailments in the same ratio. He has cured over 5000 cases of another class of diseases that is common in this country, and he has lost only one patient in 27 years.

This Great Healer has a specific for all Heart Troubles, Lungs, Liver and Kidneys. All humors of the blood pass away like a shadow, under his treatment.

If you are sick, no matter what your trouble is, be sure to see this Great Seer and Healer. Before you take medicine, find out what your disease is. Life is too precious to be dallied with, or to be guessed at. A word to the wise is sufficient. Remember this is an opportunity of a lifetime.

Office hours from 9 a. m. to 8 p. m. Sunday, 9 to 5 p. m.

DR. GRIFFIN,
THE VETERAN SEER AND HEALER.

CLEVELAND'S Superior Baking Powder.
Used and recommended by Mrs. . E. Humphrey, Teacher of Cooking.

COLD WATER CAKE.

One and a half cups sugar, a quarter cup butter, two and a half cups flour, two eggs, one cup water, two teaspoonfuls baking powder. Flavor with vanilla or lemon.

CORN STARCH CAKE.

Two cups sugar, a half cup butter, one cup sweet milk, two cups flour, one cup corn starch, whites seven eggs, beaten stiff, two tablespoonfuls baking powder. Stir the butter and sugar to a cream; sift the flour and corn starch together; add the eggs last. Mix in an earthen vessel, and flavor with lemon.

COCOANUT CAKE.

One cup sugar, a third cup butter, a half cup sweet milk, one and a half cups flour, two teaspoonfuls baking powder, whites of three eggs beaten to a froth, and added last. Stir very little after the eggs are in.

FILLING.—The rind and juice of one lemon, yolk one egg, one cup powdered sugar, a half cocoanut grated and a little milk; cook until thick.

FROSTING.—Three tablespoonfuls powdered sugar, white of one egg, and the other half of the cocoanut.

COCOANUT CAKE.

Three quarters cup butter, two cups sugar, yolks four eggs and whites of two, one cup sweet milk, three and a half cups flour, two teaspoonfuls baking powder. Bake in jelly tins. Grate one fresh cocoanut, or use dessicated cocoanut soaked in milk and drained. Cover the layers with boiled icing and sprinkle thickly with cocoanut.

OUR SPEIRS' SPECIAL LADIES' MACHINE is an elegant bicycle, and we ask you to see it before buying. 279 MAIN STREET.

SPEIRS' MFG. CO.

CLEANSING AND DYEING
AT THE
NAPHTHA ✢ LAUNDRY,
49 GARDNER STREET.

Office until May 1st at 96 FRONT ST., and then notice the display of Dyeing and Cleansing at our

NEW OFFICE, 541 MAIN STREET,
FRANKLIN SQUARE.

Whole or ripped Garments, Laces, Draperies, Embroidered Goods, Shawls and Blankets, Furniture, Bedding and Carpets.

See our Descriptive Circular and Price List. Address NAPHTHA LAUNDRY, Worcester, Mass. by mail or telephone.

CHAS. C. MINSCH,

Fresco Painter and Decorator.

AGENCY FOR
METAL CEILINGS.

Office,
No. 12 Pearl Street,   **WORCESTER, MASS.**

Cleveland's Superior Baking Powder.
Used and recommended by Mrs. C. E. Humphrey, Teacher of Cooking.

ALMOND CAKE.

Three-quarters cup butter, one cup sugar, half cup sweet milk, three eggs, whites and yolks beaten separately, two cups flour, two level teaspoonfuls baking powder, and one pound almonds blanched and sliced, stirred in last. Save a few whole ones to put on top of icing.

ALMOND CAKE.

Two cups sugar, a half cup butter, three fourths cup sweet milk, whites eight eggs, three even cups flour, one and a half teaspoonfuls baking powder two teaspoonfuls bitter almonds.

ANGEL CAKE.

Whites eleven eggs, one and a half cups granulated sugar, sifted once, one cup flour sifted with one teaspoonful cream of tartar four times, one teaspoonful vanilla. Bake in an ungreased pan forty minutes. When done invert pan on two cups and let stand until cake is cold.

CHOCOLATE LAYER CAKE.

One cup sugar, half cup butter, two eggs, half cup sweet milk, two cups flour, two teaspoonfuls baking powder.
Filling.—Half cake chocolate grated and dissolved in a small cup milk; let boil and then add a half cup sugar, small piece butter, a little salt and flavoring.

COFFEE CAKE.

Half cup butter, one cup brown sugar, one cup molasses, one cup strong coffee (boiled) one beaten egg, four cups flour, one heaping teaspoonful baking powder, one tablespoonful cinnamon, one teaspoonful cloves, two pounds seedless raisins, a quarter pound sliced citron. Dredge the fruit and add last. Bake one hour.

Baker's Extracts are used exclusively by the United States Government in the National Homes.

EUREKA MFG. CO.

Manufacturers of Ladies', Misses', Children's and Youths'

✣ SHOES. ✣

Office and Salesroom, 44 Southbridge St.

WORCESTER, MASS.

Opp. the New Postoffice.

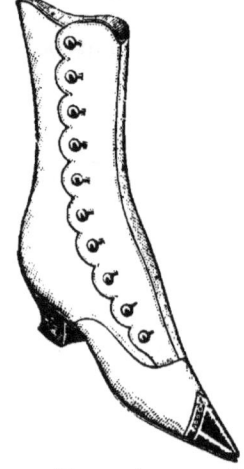

We wish to call your attention to the fact that we make a full line of Button, Lace and Oxford Shoes in genuine Dongola and Russet Leather, which for solidity, style and sterling wearing qualities, are unsurpassed by any in New England.

We are prepared to fit you on any style, all widths, from C to EE, Narrow Opera Toe, Opera Toe, Square Toe and Common Sense, plain or Pat. Tip Toe, at prices ranging from $1.00 to $1.50 for Ladies' Button or Lace, Oxfords from 75 cts to $1.25, Misses' Button or Lace from 85 cts to $1.25, Childrens' Button or Lace, sizes 5 to 10, from 60c to $1.00, Youths' Lace, 11 to 2, 85c to $1.25.

These goods are sold at Manufacturers' Prices, therefore you save two profits, the Jobber's and the Retail Merchant's.

Give us a trial and save money. All goods warranted to give satisfaction or money refunded.

Every shoe you buy will cost from 25 to 50 cts less than you would pay in any store in the city.

Remember the address, where you will find us every hour of the day, every day of the week, Saturday night till 10 o'clock.

44 SOUTHBRIDGE ST., opp. New P. O.

EUREKA MFG. CO.,

JAMES MILNES, Treas.

CLEVELAND'S Superior Baking Powder.

Used and recommended by Mrs. C. E. Humphrey, Teacher of Cooking.

CITRON POUND CAKE.

Three quarters pound butter rubbed to a cream with one pound sugar. Add first the beaten yolks eight large or ten small eggs, then one pound flour, beaten whites of the eggs and last one and a quarter pounds finely selected citron slightly dredged with flour. Bake one and a half or two hours.

CENTENNIAL WASHINGTON CAKE.

Three quarters pound butter, one and a half pounds brown sugar, six eggs, whites and yolks beaten separately, one pint sweet milk, one and three-quarters pounds flour and two teaspoonfuls baking powder. Three quarters pound currants, washed and dried, a quarter pound raisins, (stoned), a quarter pound citron, sliced, one grated nutmeg, one wine glass wine. Sprinkle fruit with part of flour. Cream the butter with the sugar, add beaten yolks, wine, milk, nutmeg and flour and whites of eggs alternately. Put in fruit last, mix well and bake one hour and three-quarters. An old and excellent receipt.

DELICATE CAKE.

Three quarters cup butter, rubbed to a cream, with two cups sugar, half cup sweet milk, three cups flour, one and a half teaspoonfuls baking powder, whites of eight eggs, well beaten. Add flour and eggs alternately. Flavor.

POUND CAKE.

Yolks of ten eggs, whites of two well beaten. One pound butter, one pound sugar, one pound flour, one and a half teaspoonfuls baking powder, one cup milk. Add flour and whites last.

BICYCLE RIDING SCHOOL. We have the only school in this section, at Worcester Skating Rink.
SPEIRS MFG. CO. 279 Main St. LINCOLN HOLLAND, Manager.

GARFIELD & HARRINGTON,
Quinsigamond Lake Ice.

DEALERS IN

⇢ COAL ⇠

Furniture Moving and Teaming of all kinds.

OFFICE, 96 SCHOOL ST.,

WORCESTER, - MASS.

Ice

The old and reliable firm.
Wholesale and Retail Dealers.

Walker Ice Co.

Office, No. 25 Exchange St.,
Worcester, Mass.

Ice

Cleveland's Superior Baking Powder.
Used and recommended by Mrs. C. E. Humphrey, Teacher of Cooking.

CINNAMON CHOCOLATE CAKE.

Half cup butter, one cup granulated sugar, two eggs well beaten, half cup sweet milk, one and a half cups flour, one and a half teaspoonfuls baking powder, three teaspoonfuls cinnamon. Cream the butter, then add gradually the sugar, beaten eggs, milk, and a very little salt. When all is well beaten together add the spice.

CHOCOLATE FILLING FOR ABOVE.—Whites of two eggs and confectioners sugar beaten together to the consistency of icing, but not too stiff. One ounce (or a square) of chocolate dissolved on stove in a small pan. When melted pour into icing and mix thoroughly. This makes a two-layer cake.

MARBLED CHOCOLATE CAKE.

Half cup butter and a cup sugar beaten to a cream, a half cup sweet milk, one and a half cups flour, one teaspoonful baking powder, whites four eggs added last. Take one cup this mixture and add to it five tablespoonfuls grated chocolate wet with milk and flavor with vanilla. Put a layer of white batter in cake pan, drop the chocolate batter with a spoon in spots; pour over the remaining white batter and bake. Ice with chocolate icing.

COFFEE CAKE.

A half cup butter, one cup brown sugar, one cup molasses, one cup strong coffee (boiled), one beaten egg, four cups flour, one heaping teaspoonful baking powder, one tablespoonful cinnamon, one teaspoonful cloves, two pounds seedless raisins, a quarter pound sliced citron. Dredge the fruit and add last. Bake one hour.

BICYCLE SUNDRIES, Parts and Repairs. A call will satisfy all interested that we can supply all wants.
276 MAIN STREET. SPEIRS MFG. Co.

JOHN A. HARTIGAN,

DEALER IN

Staple and Fancy

GROCERIES,

Sunshine Flour, Walker Butter, Peterboro Butter, Mrs. Streeter's Home-Made Cake, University Coffee, Perfectly Pure Spices, Mammoth Queen Olives, Orange Pekoe Tea.

JERSEY CREAM, FRESH EVERY DAY.

HIGH GRADE
Teas and Coffees,
CONDIMENTS, CIGARS, ETC.

Headquarters for Mineral Waters.

JOHN A. HARTIGAN,
305 MAIN STREET,
WORCESTER, - MASS.

Cleveland's Superior Baking Powder.

Used and recommended by Mrs. C. E. Humphrey, Teacher of Cooking.

FROSTING.

Allow ten teaspoonfuls powdered sugar and a half teaspoonful lemon juice to the white of one egg. Beat the egg till you can invert a teaspoonful without its falling, then beat in the sugar, a teaspoonful at a time, add the lemon juice, and spread upon the warm cake with a broad knife dipped occasionally in cold water. Put in a cool, dry place to harden. If the cake is rich, dust with flour, brushing afterwards lightly with a napkin to remove what does not adhere, before frosting it.

SOFT FROSTING.

One cup granulated sugar, a half cup milk. Let boil till it drops from spoon in strings. Pour into a bowl and add one teaspoonful flour. Beat a few moments and let stand till cool and thick enough to spread on cake without running.

GELATINE FROSTING.

A teaspoonful gelatine soaked till soft in one tablespoonful cold water and dissolved in two tablespoonfuls boiling water. Strain into a small bowl, and add enough powdered sugar to make it spread easily on the cake. Flavor with a few drops of vanilla.

FLOATING ISLAND.

Make a custard of the yolks six eggs, one quart milk, a pinch of salt, sugar to taste. Pour into a large dish. Beat whites to a stiff froth, and put by spoonfuls, in boiling water, turn them carefully till cooked. Take out with a skimmer and put on top of custard. Serve ice cold.

OUR BICYCLES, we claim, are equal to any made, and are "Built in this City." This IS of importance.

SPEIRS MFG. CO.,
279 MAIN STREET, - WORCESTER.

CHICKERING PIANOS

THE WORLD'S STANDARD PIANO.

S. R. LELAND & SON,

Dealers in Pianos and Organs, from the standard factories only. Sheet Music and General Musical Merchandise. Tuning, Repairing, Polishing, or Moving of Pianos. Instruments of all kinds rented or sold on easy instalments.

446 MAIN ST.

If You Want a Piano,

CHICKERING PIANOS

BUY THE BEST.

CLEVELAND'S SUPERIOR BAKING OWDER.
Used and recommended by Mrs. C. E. Humphrey, Teacher of Cooking.

SOFT GINGERBREAD.

One cup molasses, half cup sugar, half cup butter, half cup sweet milk, two eggs, a tablespoonful ginger, one teaspoonful allspice, two cups flour sifted with one and a half teaspoonfuls baking powder. Bake in shallow pan, or small pans.

SOFT GINGERBREAD.

One small half cup butter, one and a half cups molasses, two well beaten eggs, three cups flour, one tablespoonful ginger, a little each of nutmeg, allspice and cinnamon, a half cup sweet milk, one and a half teaspoonfuls baking powder.

SPONGE GINGERBREAD.

Mix one cup molasses, a half cup melted butter, one tablespoonful ginger; make them quite warm, and add one teaspoonful soda, then one cup sour milk, two eggs beaten, and flour to make like pound cake.

HICKORY NUT KISSES.

Whites of six eggs beaten stiff, one pound powdered sugar, two tablespoonfuls flour, and one pound hickory nut kernels. Drop on well buttered tins, and bake in a moderate oven.

CREAM PUFFS.

A half cup butter melted in one cup hot water; put in a small tin pan on the stove to boil; while boiling stir in a cup flour; take off and let cool; when cold stir in three eggs, one after the other, without beating. Drop on buttered tins and bake in a hot oven twenty to thirty minutes.

FILLING.—One cup milk, one egg, a half cup sugar; thicken with corn starch and flavor with vanilla.

We have a full line of Out Door Goods of all description, a nice store, and cordially invite you to call at 279 MAIN STREET.
LINCOLN HOLLAND, Manager.

EDWIN HAWES

AGENT FOR THE

"VOLUNTEER"

AND

"ALL RIGHT"

Steam and Hot Water Boilers,

REFERENCES.

VOLUNTEER.	ALL RIGHT.
Dr. J. K. Warren,	Mrs. J. C. Mattoon,
John E. Day,	John E. Day,
O. W. Norcross,	C. F. Stevens,
H. H. Bigelow,	C. H. Goodell,
F. H. Pelton,	F. S. Blanchard,
H. L. Miller.	H. E. Hall,

EDWIN HAWES, 246 Main Street, Worcester, Mass.

ARTISTIC HANGINGS.

MISS H. A. SMITH,

Agent for the Associated Artists, New York.

Draperies, Canopies, etc. made and put up. Houses and Rooms Decorated and Furnished complete when desired. Choice pieces China and Glass always on hand.

10 HARVARD STREET, WORCESTER.

Artistic Dressmaking,

AT REASONABLE RATES, AT

MRS. A. SPENCER'S

61 PLEASANT STREET.

UP ONE FLIGHT.

MISS K. A. MULLANEY, LADIES' HAIR DRESSING, HYGIENIC FACE STEAMING and Massage Parlors. Room 9 Burnside Building. FIRST FLOOR.

CHOCOLATE ICE CREAM.

One quart cream, one pint milk, two cups sugar, two eggs beaten light, five tablespoonfuls grated chocolate, rubbed smooth in a little milk. Heat milk to near boiling, pour in slowly beaten eggs and sugar, then the chocolate. Cook till it thickens, stirring constantly. Cool, beat in the cream, and freeze.

FRUIT ICE CREAM.

One generous pint milk, two cups sugar, one small tablespoonful flour, two eggs, two tablespoonfuls gelatine soaked in a little cold water, a quart cream, four bananas, half a pound candied cherries, and other fruit, if desired. Let milk come to a boil, beat flour, sugar and eggs together and stir in boiling milk. Cook twenty minutes, then add gelatine. When cold add cream. Put in freezer, freeze ten minutes, add cup of fruit, and finish freezing.

PINEAPPLE ICE CREAM.

Three pints cream, one pint milk, two ripe pineapples, two pounds sugar. Slice pineapples thin, scatter sugar over them, and let it stand three hours. Cut or chop the fruit into the syrup and strain through a bag of coarse lace. Beat gradually into the cream, and freeze. Remove a few bits of pineapple, and stir in cream when half frozen. Peach ice cream made in the same way is delicious.

FROZEN MILK PUNCH.

Freeze together one quart milk and a half pound sugar. After the above is frozen mix with it a half pint rum, a half pint brandy, one and a half pints whipped cream and half a nutmeg.

Hotel Adams. Finest Rooms and Best Board in the City, for the money.

HAVE YOUR CARPETS DUSTED AT THE

Worcester Carpet Dusting Works,

J. C. WATERS, PROPRIETOR.

Carpets and Furniture Cleansed by the Naphtha Process. The only Place in the city where Hot Naphtha is used. Carpets called for and delivered, and taken up and relaid.

FEATHERS RENOVATED BY STEAM,
and made as Light and Good as New.

☞ TAKE NOTICE.—All orders should be left at Bemis & Co.'s Shoe Store, 423 Main St., or addressed to J. C. WATERS.

CURTIS STREET,   NEW WORCESTER.
TELEPHONE, 347-5.

PRICE LIST—For Taking Up Carpet, 1 c per yd. For Dusting Carpet, 3 cts per yd. For Laying Carpet, 3 cts per yd. Naphtha Cleansing Ingrain, 8 cts per yd. Naphtha Cleansing Brussells and Tapestry, 10 cts per yd. Renovating Feather Bed, $2, Washing Tick, 25 cts. Making Over Hair Mattress, $2.50. New Mattress Tick, $2.50. New Tick for Feathers, $2. Second Hand Carpets Bought and Sold.

CAN U BY SHEWS BET HER OR CHEAP HER THAN OF ME.

CALL AND SEE ME AT
630 MAIN STREET.

Have the best line of

SHOES

in the city, for the money.

Special attention given to Ladies' and Gents' Repairing, using the best stock, and all work guaranteed.

W. A. RICE, 630 Main St.

CLEVELAND'S SUPERIOR BAKING POWDER.
Used and recommended by Mrs. C. E. Humphrey, Teacher of Cooking.

SPICE DROP CAKES.

Yolks three eggs, one half cup shortening, one cup molasses, half cup sweet milk, three cups flour, two teaspoonfuls baking powder. Spice with nutmeg, cinnamon, cloves, and flavor with lemon. Drop on buttered paper on tins, and bake very quickly.

WALNUT WAFERS.

A half pound brown sugar, half pound walnut meats, slightly broken but not chopped, three even tablespoonfuls flour, a fourth teaspoonful baking powder, a third teaspoonful salt, two eggs; beat the eggs, add the sugar, salt, flour, and lastly meats. Drop small spoonfuls on buttered pans, and bake till brown. Remove from pans as soon as baked. Butternut meats are also nice.

BOILED ICING.

Boil one cup granulated sugar with four tablespoonfuls water until it drops from spoon in threads. Have ready the beaten white one egg, and pour the syrup slowly into it, beating all the time. Flavor. Spread on cake while warm.

BOILED CHOCOLATE ICING.

One cup powdered sugar, a quarter cake chocolate, (shaved), two tablespoonfuls boiling water, white of one egg. Cook a third of the sugar, the chocolate and water together until smooth. Have egg and remainder of sugar beaten together and pour into it the hot chocolate. Beat well and spread over cake at once.

HOTEL ADAMS. Elevator, all Modern Improvements. Board by Day or Week.

Worcester County Creamery,

11 MYRTLE ST.

GOFF & ROGERS, Proprietors.

Wholesale and Retail Dealers in

Milk, Butter, Cream and Eggs.

THE FINEST GOODS ONLY.

A Trial Order Solicited.

GEORGE A. COBURN,

PAINE ST., Rear 166 Lincoln St.

HIGHEST GRADE WORK IN SHIRTS, COLLARS AND CUFFS.

A Number One place to get your Lace Curtains and Blankets Laundered, also Family Work.

CLEVELAND'S SUPERIOR BAKING POWDER.
Used and recommended by Mrs. C. E. Humphrey, Teacher of Cooking.

ICE CREAM FROM CONDENSED MILK.

One can condensed milk, three tablespoonfuls corn starch, one tablespoonful extract vanilla. Add sufficient boiling water to one can of condensed milk to make it the proper consistency. Moisten three tablespoonfuls corn starch with a little cold milk, add it to the mixture, stir and cook for five minutes until smooth, take it from the fire, and when cold add vanilla extract to flavor. Freeze as directed.

ALMOND ICE CREAM.

Yolks six eggs, one quart cream, two ounces Jordan almonds, ten ounces sugar. Blanch the almonds and chop them very fine. Put two tablespoonfuls granulated sugar with the chopped almonds in a saucepan, stir over the fire until the almonds are a red brown color, take from the fire, and when cool pound them to a paste. Put the cream in a farina boiler. Beat the eggs and sugar together until light, add them to the hot cream, stir till the eggs thicken, take from fire, add the pounded almonds, and when cool add a gill of noyau, and freeze the same as ordinary ice cream.

APRICOT ICE CREAM.

One quart can apricots, a pint water, a pound sugar, a quart cream, three tablespoonfuls maraschino, yolks fourteen eggs. Put the sugar and water on to boil; boil five minutes, and skim. Beat the yolks of the eggs together until creamy, add to them the hot syrup, beat until the consistency of sponge cake batter, add the cream and maraschino, and freeze. When frozen add the apricots pressed through a fine sieve, mix, repack, and stand aside for two hours. Serve cut into blocks and placed on small napkins.

HOTEL ADAMS. Best Family Hotel in the city. Call and see for yourself.

WALL PAPERS.

Come where you can buy Paper cheap. New Store, New Goods. All the latest styles in colorings, in Wall and Ceiling Papers, also Picture Moulding and Window Shades.

Having had twenty-five years' experience as a practical Paper-Hanger with the Clark Sawyer Co., I feel confident I can give perfect satisfaction. All work done in a superior manner.

FRANKLIN A. CARR, 150 CHANDLER STREET, NEAR QUEEN.

GEO. WILMOT,
Furniture and Piano Moving,
AND STORAGE.

Personal Attention given to Shipping and Packing Goods.

━━━ FREIGHTING. ━━━

OFFICE, 153 MAIN STREET, - WORCESTER, MASS.

House and Stables, 82 Lincoln St. Telephone, 253-5.

BICKFORD & SWEET,
MANUFACTURERS OF THE CELEBRATED

"Excello" & "Perfection" Lambs' Wool Soles,
(PATENTED,) ALSO

Womens', Misses' and Childs' Hand Crotcheted Worsted Slippers, in all sizes and colors. Womens', Misses' and Childs' Eiderdown Chamois Slippers, in many beautiful colors, with patented soles, also Soft Bed Socks, finished in elegant style. One never need have cold feet. We also make a new Polishing Mitten for polishing stoves, cleaning furniture, rubbing the flesh where circulation is low. These are made from the best Lamb Skins, and no lady should be without these Mittens. Hands always clean by their use. Send twenty-five cents for one of these mittens. For further particulars, send for catalogue and prices.

BICKFORD & SWEET,
9 Washington Square, Worcester, Mass.

Cleveland's Superior Baking Powder.
Used and recommended by Mrs. C. E. Humphrey, Teacher of Cooking.

VANILLA ICE CREAM.

Two quarts rich cream, one pint new milk, one pound sugar, and one teaspoonful vanilla. Mix well and freeze.

ANOTHER WAY.—Put milk and one cut vanilla bean on fire and boil slowly. Strain through a wire sieve and when cool add cream and sugar, and freeze.

LEMON ICE.

One quart water, one tablespoonful corn starch; boil till all taste of starch is gone. Add the lemon (two large lemons to a quart). Sweeten to taste when the mixture is cold, and leave the rind in for a while. Strain through a sieve and freeze.

JUNKET.

Sweeten to taste one quart fresh milk, stir in a tablespoonful liquid rennet, and pour into a glass dish. Set near the stove where it will get warm, and as soon as it begins to thicken, set on ice. Serve with preserves and cream. Excellent for invalids.

STRAWBERRY ICE CREAM.

A half pound strawberry jam, a half pound strawberries, a half pound sugar, one pint cream, a half pint new milk. Mash the strawberries and add them to the strawberry jam. Add the sugar to the cream, stir until dissolved, add the milk, and freeze. When frozen stir in the strawberry mixture. Repack, and stand aside to ripen.

HOTEL ADAMS. Cor Pleasant and High Streets
Best accomomdations in the city

FARNSWORTH'S BAGGAGE TRANSFER,

CALVIN FARNSWORTH, Prop.

Office at Parcel Room, next Baggage Room, Union Passenger Station, Worcester, Mass.

Hacks and Baggage Wagons always ready. Barges and Mountain Wagons furnished for parties at reasonable prices.

FURNITURE MOVED
by Careful and Experienced Men.

STABLE, REAR OF BAY STATE HOUSE,

330  **330**

If your Eyes trouble you, call at the
OLD RELIABLE
SPECTACLE DEPOT,
Established in 1858,

and have them thoroughly tested and correctly fitted by a Scientific Optician who has had thirty years' practice.

STOCKWELL & PRATT,
Eye Specialists.

Opposite Barnard, Sumner & Putnam Co. We have been 30 years within fifty feet of our present location.

330   MAIN STREET.   330

Cleveland's Superior Baking Powder.
Used and recommended by Mrs. C. E. Humphrey, Teacher of Cooking.

APRICOT ICE CREAM.

A half pound apricot jam, a pint cream, juice one lemon, two tablespoonfuls noyau. Mix jam and cream together, then carefully add the lemon juice and noyau, strain through a fine sieve and freeze as directed for ordinary ice cream.

BROWNED BREAD ICE CREAM.

Two slices (three ounces) bread, four ounces sugar, two lady fingers, a half pint milk. a pint cream, four tablespoonfuls maraschino. Put the bread in the oven and brown to a golden color, roll and sift it. Dry and roll the lady fingers. Put the crerm, milk and sugar in a double boiler, stir until the sugar is dissolved, and when cold, freeze. When frozen add the sifted crumbs and maraschino; mix, repack and stand aside to ripen.

APRICOT SHERBET.

One quart can apricots, one lemon, a half pound sugar, a quart water. Boil sugar and water together five minutes; press apricots through a sieve. add them to the syrup, add the lemon juice, and when cold freeze the same as ice cream, then add the meringue. Peach sherbet is made in precisely the same manner.

BANANA SHERBET.

One dozen red skinned bananas, one pound sugar, two oranges, one quart water. Boil sugar and water together five minutes, take from fire and add juice of the oranges, and when cold add the bananas, mashed fine. Freeze as directed. When frozen add the meringue.

We shall be pleased to see you at any time. and extend an invitation to call and inspect our goods. SPEIRS MFG. CO., 279 MAIN ST. LINCOLN HOLLAND, Manager.

L. V. K. VAN DE MARK,
Real Estate and General Appraiser.

Mortgages Negotiated.
Money to Loan.
Tenements to Rent.

If you have property to dispose of or desire to purchase, give me a call.

476 MAIN STREET, — WORCESTER, MASS.
TAKE ELEVATOR.

GEO. S. HATCH,
New Shop, 25 Queen Street, - Worcester, Mass.
MANUFACTURER OF
Mattresses and Bedding of all Descriptions.

Special attention given to making over Hair Mattresses and Renovating Feathers. Upholstering neatly done.

COUCHES, ALSO SPRING BEDS Always in Stock.

If you cannot call, send postal and we will call upon you.

CLEVELAND'S Superior Baking Powder.
Used and recommended by Mrs. C. E. Humphrey, Teacher of Cooking.

CHOCOLATE ICE CREAM.

One quart cream, one pint milk, three-fourths pound sugar, two eggs, five tablespoonfuls chocolate. Scald the milk and add it to the sugar and eggs beaten together, and the chocolate rubbed smooth in a little milk. Beat well, place over the fire till it thickens, stirring constantly. Take from the fire, and when cool add the cream and freeze.

CHOCOLATE FRUIT ICE CREAM.

One quart cream, one pint milk, three-fourths pound sugar, two eggs, five tablespoonfuls chocolate. Make precisely the same as above, adding, when almost frozen, a cup preserved fruit cut in small pieces.

POOR MAN'S ICE CREAM.

One pint cream, one pint milk, juice one lemon, half pound sugar, half nutmeg, grated. Add the lemon juice to the sugar, then mix them with the milk and cream; add the nutmeg and freeze.

RASPBERRY ICE CREAM.

One pound raspberry jam, juice of one lemon, one pint cream, one gill milk. Mix the lemon juice with the raspberry jam, and add gradually the milk and cream; strain through a sieve and freeze.

PEACH ICE CREAM.

One quart can peaches, a pint water, a pound sugar, a quart cream, three tablespoonfuls maraschino, yolks fourteen eggs. Made precisely the same as apricot.

CLEVELAND'S Superior Baking Powder.
Used and recommended by Mrs. C. E. Humphrey, Teacher of Cooking.

Take The Great French Hospital Remedy.

One peculiarity about it is that it tastes like wine, yet contains no liquor or alcohol in any form, being a tonic, but not a stimulant. Another peculiarity is that

Blood Wine

It Cures. Cures all Nervous Disorders and all Blood, Stomach, Liver and Kidney Diseases. The price is **50 cents**, and you can get it of your druggists, and if it fails to cure, you get your money back.

Compounded only by

The Louis Daudelin Co., Worcester, Mass.

WRITE NOW FOR AGENTS' PRICES, ETC.

CHAS. E. SEBBENS

NATIVE OR WESTERN   Manufacturer and Wholesale Dealer In   HORSE RADISH ROOTS

PURE DOMESTIC PREPARED **HORSE** CLEANEST PUREST **RADISH**

Tomato Catsup, Piccalilli, Chowchow, Sauces &c.

WHITE WINE VINEGAR

Goods Bottled and in Bulk, Outfit FREE for Agents to Peddle by Measure.

OFFICE 26 LEADS FROM 134 FRONT ST. **SPRING ST.**

AGENTS WANTED IN   Orders by Mail or Express Promptly Filled.   EVERY CITY & TOWN.

WORCESTER, MASS.

GOOD PAY, NICE WORK; JUST TRY IT.

INDEX TO ADVERTISEMENTS.

	PAGE		PAGE
ARTISTIC HANGINGS		**CABINET MAKERS**	
Smith, H. A.	125	Harwood, E. A.	71
ATTORNEYS		**CARPET CLEANING**	
Brown, Adams, Franklin, front cover and foot lines.		Worcester Carpet Dusting Works,	127
Gates, William H.,	63		
Woodward, George M.,	51	**CATERERS**	
Verry, Horace B.	89	Jennison, H. W. & Co. head lines.	
BAGGAGE TRANSFER			
Farnsworth, Calvin	133	Zahonji, L. J.,	57
BAKERIES		**CHIROPODIST**	
Jennison H. W. & Co., top lines.		Carberry, Miss A. V.,	107
Morgan, F. E.,	39		
BAKING POWDER		**CLAIRVOYANTS**	
Cleveland's, top lines.		Irvano Millie,	2
BANKS		**CLAVIERS**	
Co-opertive Banks,	69	Wilder, H. S.,	53
People's Savings Bank,	9	**CLOAKS**	
Wor. Co. Inst. for Savings, page 3 cover		Healy, Richard,	4
Worcester Five cent Savings bank	9	Paris Cloak and Suit Store.	2
Worcester Mechanics Savings Bank,	5	**CLOCK REPAIRER**	
		Randall, N. L.,	111
Worcester Safe Deposit Trust Co.	85	Garfield & Harrington,	119
BATHS		**CLOTHING**	
Jensen's, head and foot lines.		Eames, D. H. & Co., first cover	
BICYCLES		**COAL**	
Lowe, John A.	47	Sumner, E. A.,	7
Speirs Mfg Co, foot lines.		Wellington, Fred W. & Co.,	35
BOILERS		**COFFEE**	
Hawes, Edwin,	125	Howe, D. A., head lines	
BOOK BINDING		**CONFECTIONERY**	
		Livingstone's,	61
Wesby, J. S. and Sons,	71	Oxley, F. N.,	77

Albert H. Bloss.
Geo. W. Rousseau. **Worcester Rubber Company,**
Wholesale and Retail Dealers in **RUBBER GOODS**

INDEX TO ADVERTISEMENTS—CONTINUED.

CORSETS
Worcester Corset Co., 29

CRACKERS
Stearns, 37

CREAMERIES
Worcester Co. Creamery, 129

DRESS MAKING
Bean, Miss R. E., 41
Cole, Miss Emma A., 33
Frazier, Miss A., 63
Spencer, A., 125

DRY GOODS
Barnard, Sumner, Putnam Co., 21
Clarke, J. H. & Co., 1

DYE HOUSE
LeJolly Dye House, 4

DYSPEPSIA CURE
Bardwell, 99

EDUCATIONAL
Bowen, Mrs. foot lines.
School of English Speech, 93
Walch, Mrs. L. F. 25

ELASTIC GARMENTS
Scott, Lewis H., 93

ELECTRICIANS
Hubbard & Ham, front cover

ELECTROPLATING
Acme Plating Works, 59
Bay State Plating Co., 77
Burwell, A. B , 91
Globe Plating Co., 111

EMPLOYMENT AGENCY
Mulvey, Mrs. M. C., 27

ENGRAVERS
Lindfors, C. T., 55

EXTRACTS
Baker's, foot lines
Jennison, George, 101

FISH
Baker, Witherell & Co., 17

FLOUR
B. M C., head lines
Rogers, George & Co., front cover
Gray, ArthurE., 95
Hoppin, George S. & Co., 31
Stevens, George A., 99

FURNITURE MOVING
Wilmot, George, 131

FLY KILLER MFRS
Bigelow, J. F. 103

FURNITURE
Gately & Rogers Furniture Co. 37
Kendal, Horace & Sons, 23
Loring, J. W. & Son, 97
Putnam & Sprague Co., 19

FURNITURE FINISHER
Goodspeed, E. B. 57

GAS
Worcester Gas Light Co., 109

GROCERIES and MEATS
Grand Central Market, 49
Hartigan, John A., 121
Minckler, C. E., 39

HAIR DRESSING
Bond, Mise J. F. (Emporium) 41
Moriarty, Miss, 93

HATTERS and FURRIERS
Kendall, John & Co., 67

ICE
Garfield & Harrington, 119
Walker Ice Co., 119

INSURANCE
Munroe, A. C., 73

JEWELERS
Gard, T. D., head and foot lines
Pennington, L. W., 51

INDEX TO RECIPES.

	PAGE			PAGE
Beef, Braised	78	Cake, Cream		46
Biscuit, Cheese	38	" Delicate		118
" Egg	32	" Drop		128
" Milk	48	" Dutch Apple		52
" Quaker	52	" Indian		60
" Tea	50	" Fruit		40
Bread,	52	" Jelly		56
" Corn	50	" Marbled		120
" Cherry or Blackberry,	112	" Pound		118
" Derbyshire	32	" Short		20
Buns, Hygenic	38	" Southern Gold Loaf		42
Cake, Almond	26	" Snow Cocoanut		54
" Angel	40 and 116	" Spice		34
" Almond,	116	" Sponge		34
" Bakestone	48	" Tea	50 and	60
" Berwick Sponge	44	" White Fruit		54
" Bread	46	Clam Batter,		76
" Centennial	118	Chops, French		14
" Chocolate Layer	116	Croquette, Potato		18
" Chocolate	110	DESSERTS.		
" Cinnamon	119	Ambrosia,		28
" Citron Pound	118	Apple Snow,		94
" Cold Water	114	Bananas, Baked		78
" Corn Starch	114	Charlotte Russe,		94
" Coffee	116 and 120	Cream, Almond		26
" Cocoanut	114	" Bavarian		100

FOR CHILDREN WHILE CUTTING THEIR TEETH. AN OLD AND WELL TRIED REMEDY.

For over Fifty Years Mrs. Winslow's Soothing Syrup has been used by millions of mothers for their children while teething, with perfect success. It sooths the child, softens the gums, allays all pain; cures wind colic, and is the best remedy for diarrhœa. Sold by druggists in every part of the world. Be sure and ask for Mrs. Winslow's Soothing Syrup, and take no other kind. Twenty-five cts. a bottle.

INDEX TO RECIPES—CONTINUED.

Cream, Bohemian	100	
" Orange	30	
" Russian	100	
" Spanish	104	
" Strawberry	104	
" Strawberry or Raspberry Sponge	98	
Dressing, Boiled Salad	92	
" Cream	92	
" French	86	
" Mayonnaise	86	
" Poultry or Meat	78	
Eggs, Omelet	10	
" Scotch	10	
French Rusk,	56	
Floating Island	122	
Frosting	122	
" soft	122	
" gelatine	122	
Fish, a la Cream	72	
" Baked	16	
" Baked Halibut	68	
" Halibut au Gratin	12	
" " Balls	74	
" Salt Cod Stewed	66	
" Smelts Fried	62	
Fritters, Clam	76	
" Tomato	18	
Frosting, Boiled	34	
Gingerbread, New York	28	
" Soft	124	
" Sponge	124	
Ginger Snaps,	50 and 56	

Ham Balls,	82
Hermits,	28
Hickory Nut Kisses	124
Ice Cream 126, 130, 132 134, 136	
Jelly, Irish Moss	30
Lamb, Fricassee	80
Lemonade,	30
Lobster Cream,	68
" In Aspic	70
Meat, Smothered	84
Muffins,	38
" Cream	60
" Hominy,	38
Mutton, Curry	88
" Hash	82
Onions, Scalloped	14
Oysters, a la Thorndike	70
" Broiled	12
" Deviled	66
" calloped	74
" Smothered or Fancy Roast	66
Pastry, Plain	20
Pie, Apple	108
Pie, Lemon	20
Pop Overs,	44
Pork Tenderloin,	82
Porridge, Plum	24
Potatoes, au Gratin	36
" Balls	36
" Scalloped	36

W. A. ENGLAND, Watch and Jewelry Repairing promptly done.
394 MAIN ST.   Sign at the Sidewalk.

INDEX TO ADVERTISEMENTS—CONTINUED.

KODAKS
Worcester Supply Co.   87

LAUNDRIES
Standard,   53

LOANS
Currier, J.L., head and foot lines

LOCKSMITH
Cummings, Charles A.   71

LUNCH ROOMS
Marshal, F. E. & W. E., head lines

MANICURE
Rice, Carrie Frances,   49

MATTRESSES
Griffin, John J.,   105
Hatch, George S.,   135
Hyland Wm. & Son,   33

MEDICINE
Blood Wine,   138

MILLINERY
Doherty, Miss M. A.   101
Green, Mrs. H. A.,   49
Kessell's,   27
Pratt, Mrs. L. A.   111

OPTICIANS
Stockwell & Pratt,   133

ORATORY and MUSIC
Worcester School of Oratory and Music   45

OVERGAITERS
Eddy, Ella H.,   21

PAINTS
Atherton Paint Co.,   79
Lowell, C. C.,   47

PAINTERS
Holt, L. B.,   69
Minsch, Charles C.   115

PHYSICIANS
Dr. Griffin,   113

PICTURE FRAMES
Boutelle, G. S. & Co., front cover

PHOTOGRAPHERS
Blair, C. L.,   6
Hevy,   43
Lawrence,   107
Webster,   91

PIANOS
Gorham, C. L. & Co.,   11
Leland, S. R. & Son,   123

PLUMBERS
Cahill J. T.,   55
Greene, J. W.,   31
Middlemas, Chas. A.,   101
Sisson, J. D.   89

PROPRIETARY EXTRACTS and TOILET GOODS
Elklund, C. A. & Co., foot lines

REAL ESTATE
Broad, O. G. & Co., front cover
Van de Mark, L. V. K.   135
Garbutt, Wm. & Co., front cover

REFRIGERATORS
The Clark Sawyer Co.   cover 2

RUBBER GOODS
Worcester Rubber Co.   140

RUBBER STAMPS
Frost Stamp and Ink Works,   59

SEWING MACHINES
Eureka Mfg Co.   117
Percy, Miss C. L.,   111

SHOES
Healey, Richard J.,   59
Rice, W. A.   127

SKATES
The Sam'l Winslow Skate Mfg Co.   137

SOOTHING SYRUP
Mrs. Winslow's, index foot line

SPICES
Smith, E. T. & Co.   head lines

INDEX TO ADVERTISEMENTS—CONTINUED.

STATIONERY and OFFICE SUPPLIES
Lewis, William W., head and foot lines

STORAGE
Metropolitan Storage and Warerooms, 45
Worcester Storage Co., 75

STORE FIXTURES
Dalbeck, O., 93

STOVES
Boardman Bros., 69
Jordan, J. W., 3
Kendall, O. S. & Co., 13

TABLE DELICACIES
Sebbens, Charles E. 138

TICKET AGENTS
Rawson, Simpson & Co. front cover

TOWEL SUPPLY
Union Clean Towel Supply Co. 87

TRUNKS
Barr, George L., 51

UNDERTAKERS
Reynolds & Murphy, 61

UPHOLSTERERS
Derby, C. H. & Co., 103
White & Osterburg, 95

WALL PAPERS
Carr, Franklin A. 131
Borman, C. G., 97
Higgins E. G. Co., 15
Peterson, T. A. Co. 81

WINDOW AND DOOR SCREENS
Bemis, A. L., 63

WOOD and KINDLINGS
Warren, J. C., 57

WOOL SOLES
Beckford & Sweet, 131

WOOLEN MFRS
Valley Woolen Mill, 83

INDEX TO RECIPES—CONTINUED.

Puddings,	Arrowroot	22	Sauce, Drawn Butter		76
"	Boston	112	" Hollandaise		16
"	Brown Betty	112	" Lobster		72
"	Cabinet	24	" Mushroom		80
"	Dutch Apple	108	Sausage, Beef		84
"	Prune	22 and 106	" Mutton		88
"	Peach	106	Sherbet, Orange		26
"	Cottage	106	" Apricot		134
"	Snow	106	" Banana		134
"	Steamed Berry	108	Souffle, Cheese		12
"	Cream	124	" Chicken		14
Puffs, Orange		110	" Fish		16
Rarebit, Welsh		10 and 72	Soup, Italienne		4
Rice, Savory		18	Soup, Baked Bean	4 and 58
Rolls, Baking Powder		8	" Cream of Halibut		58
" Parker House		8	" Crecy,		4
" Zephyr		60	" Duchess		64
			" Onion		8
Salad, Cabbage		96	" Potato	6 and 62
" Chicken		92	" Poulette		6
" Lobster,		96	" Salmon		6
" Oyster		90	" Spring		58
" Salmon		90	Steaks, Hamburg		80
" Spinach		90			
" Tomato		90	Veal Loaf,		88
Sandwich, Salad		96			
Sauce, Brown		78 and 80	Wafers, Virginia		48
" Cream		98	" Water		44
" Foamy Egg		24	" Walnut,		128
" French		102	Waffles, Corn Meal		42
" Hard		102			
" Lemon		22 and 102	MISCELLANEOUS		
" Orange		110			
" Plain		108	Boiled Icing		128
" Pudding		98	Boiled Chocolate Icing		128
" Strawberry		108	Cannelon,		84
" Tartan		62	Clam Soup with Poached Egg	64
" White		68	Oysters and Tripe,		74
" Wine		112	Substitute for Cream,		98

J. H. CLARKE & CO.

OUR MARKED SPECIALTIES.

Silk Dress Goods,
Wool Dress Goods,
Cotton Dress Goods.

BEST EQUIPPED AND LIGHTED

BLACK DRESS GOODS DEPARTMENT

IN CENTRAL MASSACHUSETTS.

Always in stock the Choicest Production of the New and Old World-Best manufacturers only represented, including

PRIESTLEY AND LUPIN.

Recognized Leaders and Authority on

Ladies' Outside Wear and Suits,

as our GARMENT DEPARTMENT is the TALK OF THE TOWN.

Headquarters for

DOMESTICS, LINENS AND COTTONS.

Only first-class goods kept at price of medium and cheap merchandise sold elsewhere, as the best is none too good for our trade.

J. H. CLARKE & CO.

Cheapest place in Worcester to buy your CLOAKS AND FURS is the
PARIS CLOAK AND SUIT STORE, 496 Main Street.

WORCESTER
FAMILY
COOK BOOK

"THE HOUSEWIFE'S AID."

RECIPES
OF THE
WORCESTER COOKING SCHOOLS,

To which are appended other Choice Recipes.

O. F. RAWSON,
..... 391 Main Street, Worcester, Mass.,
IS OFFICIAL TICKET AGENT BOSTON & ALBANY R. R.
Tickets Sold and Berths Reserved to all points. Agent for Gaze's Excursions to all parts of the world. Agent for all Ocean and Coast Steamship Lines. Summer and Winter Excursion Tickets in their season.

WORCESTER
FAMILY COOK BOOK.

RECIPES OF
Worcester Cooking Schools,
TO WHICH ARE APPENDED
OTHER CHOICE RECIPES.

WE ARE The Popular Picture Framers
G. S. BOUTELLE & CO., of Worcester,
82 FOSTER STREET. WORCESTER, MASS.

HUBBARD & HAM, 3 Austin St., ELECTRICIANS.

GEO. P. ROGERS, 139 FRONT STREET, WORCESTER, DEALER IN The Best Family Flours, Etc.

CLOTHING.
The Finest to be had, can always be found on our counters, at prices within the reach of all.
CHILDRENS' CLOTHING A SPECIALTY.
Money returned, if for any reason a purchase is not satisfactory.
D. H. EAMES & CO.,
Main Street, cor. Front, - WORCESTER.

A. G. BROAD & CO., Real Estate, 34 Front St. Real Estate Mortgages placed at Lowest Rates.

The Alaska Refrigerator.

ELEVENTH SEASON.

For ten years we have handled the New England end of the "ALASKA" business.
For ten years the business has shown a marked increase from year to year.
For ten years the goods have steadily advanced in quality and been in the lead in the race for popularity.
There is but one best refrigerator, its name is

"ALASKA."

306,709 IN USE.

POINTS

All goods shipped from Worcester.
All orders shipped the day received.
Exclusive sales and ample protection, to insure you a profit.
A postal to-night brings your refrigerator to-morrow.
An ironclad guarantee with every one sold.

IT COSTS NOTHING TO FIND OUT ABOUT THE "ALASKA."

1895 CATALOGUE NOW READY.

——✢ WRITE TO ✢——

THE CLARK-SAWYER COMPANY,

WORCESTER, MASS.

Sole Agents for New England States

WORCESTER COUNTY
Institution for Savings,

No. 13 FOSTER ST.

This is one of the oldest Savings Banks in the state, and the largest outside of Boston. It was started in 1828.

It was established for the special advantage of those who work for wages. It receives the Savings of the people, and carefully invests the money for their benefit.

A little money deposited regularly amounts in a few years to a handsome sum.

The officers are as follows :

PRESIDENT,
STEPHEN SALISBURY

VICE PRESIDENTS,

GEORGE S. HOWE, JOSEPH MASON, JOHN D. WASHBURN.

TRUSTEES.

George S. Howe,
Joseph Mason,
John D. Washburn,
Edward L. Davis,
Stephen Salisbury,
George E. Francis,
Thomas H. Gage,
A. George Bullock,
Josiah H Clarke,
Charles B. Pratt,
John W. Wetherell,
Waldo Lincoln,
Frank P. Goulding,
Lincoln N. Kinnicutt.

Jonas G. Clark,
Charles F. Aldrich,
Samuel S. Green,
Elisha D. Buffington,
Samuel C. Willis,
Leonard Wheeler,
Edward D. Thayer, Jr.,
George F. Blake, Jr.,
Edward F. Tofman,
Lyman A. Ely,
Samuel B. Woodward,
Frederick S. Pratt,
Charles G. Washburn,
William S. Jourdan.

Treasurer, CHARLES A. CHASE.

Don't

Think our establishment is perfect, and don't criticise us too severely. It is no easy task to modernize any line of business.

Our efforts have been appreciated however, in Worcester, as well as in Providence, and other New England cities in which we have been identified with the movement to a less degree indirectly.

We believe a Market, as any other store, should be pleasant and attractive.

We believe a market should above all things be clean and the atmosphere wholesome. We cannot conceive how people have so long tolerated want of neatness in the line of business that above all others requires it.

Our aim is to make our establishment a place the best ladies of Worcester like to visit, and our goods such as they enjoy to select from.

Whether we are on the right road to the fulfillment of the above principles, we are willing to leave Dear Madam, you to be the judge.

Most respectfully yours,

The Worcester Market.

Long Distance Telephone.

www.ingramcontent.com/pod-product-compliance
Lightning Source LLC
Chambersburg PA
CBHW031459160426
43195CB00010BB/1032